SHAKESPEARE MADE EASY

MODERN ENGLISH VERSION
SIDE-BY-SIDE WITH FULL ORIGINAL TEXT

The Tempest

EDITED AND RENDERED INTO MODERN ENGLISH BY
Alan Durband

First U.S. edition published 1985 by Barron's Educational Series, Inc.

Hutchinson & Co. (Publishers) Ltd
An imprint of the Hutchinson Publishing Group
17–21 Conway Street, London W1P 6JD

Hutchinson Publishing Group (Australia) Pty Ltd
PO Box 496, 16–22 Church Street, Hawthorne,
Melbourne, Victoria 3122

Hutchinson Group (NZ) Ltd
32–34 View Road, PO Box 40–086, Glenfield, Auckland 10

Hutchinson Group (SA) (Pty) Ltd
PO Box 337, Bergvlei 2012, South Africa

First published 1984

All inquiries should be addressed to:
Barron's Educational Series, Inc.
250 Wireless Boulevard
Hauppauge, NY 11788
www.barronseduc.com

ISBN-13: 978-0-8120-3603-9
ISBN-10: 0-8120-3603-4

Library of Congress Catalog Card No. 85-4001

Library of Congress Cataloging-in-Publication Data

Shakespeare, William, 1564–1616.
The tempest: modern version side-by-side with full original text.

(Shakespeare made easy)
Summary: Presents the original text of Shakespeare's play side by side with a modern version, discusses the author and the theater of his time, and provides quizzes and other study activities.
1. Shakespeare, William, 1564–1616. Tempest. 2. Shakespeare, William, 1564–1616. Study and teaching. [1. Shakespeare, William, 1564–1616. Tempest. 2. Plays 3. Shakespeare, William, 1564–1616—Study and teaching]
I. Shakespeare, William, 1564–1616. The tempest.
II. Durband, Alan. III. Title. IV. Series: Shakespeare, William, 1564–1616. Shakespeare made easy.
PR2833.A25 1985 822.3'3 85-4001
ISBN 0-8120-3603-4

PRINTED IN THE UNITED STATES OF AMERICA
30

'Reade him, therefore; and againe, and againe: And if then you do not like him, surely you are in some danger, not to understand him. . . .'

John Hemming
Henry Condell

Preface to the 1623 Folio Edition

Shakespeare Made Easy

Titles in the series

As You Like It
Hamlet
Henry IV, Part I
Julius Caesar
King Lear
Macbeth
The Merchant of Venice
A Midsummer Night's Dream
Much Ado About Nothing
Othello
Romeo and Juliet
The Taming of the Shrew
The Tempest
Twelfth Night

Contents

Introduction

Shakespeare Made Easy is intended for readers approaching the plays for the first time, who find the language of Elizabethan poetic drama an initial obstacle to understanding and enjoyment. In the past, the only answer to the problem has been to grapple with the difficulties with the aid of explanatory footnotes (often missing when they are most needed) and a stern teacher. Generations of students have complained that "Shakespeare was ruined for me at school."

Usually a fuller appreciation of Shakespeare's plays comes in later life. Often the desire to read Shakespeare for pleasure and enrichment follows from a visit to the theater, where excellence of acting and production can bring to life qualities which sometimes lie dormant on the printed page.

Shakespeare Made Easy can never be a substitute for the original plays. It cannot possibly convey the full meaning of Shakespeare's poetic expression, which is untranslatable. *Shakespeare Made Easy* concentrates on the dramatic aspect, enabling the novice to become familiar with the plot and characters, and to experience one facet of Shakespeare's genius. To know and understand the central issues of each play is a sound starting point for further exploration and development.

Discretion can be used in choosing the best method to employ. One way is to read the original Shakespeare first, ignoring the modern version – or using it only when interest or understanding flags. Another way is to read the translation first, to establish confidence and familiarity with plot and characters.

Either way, cross-reference can be illuminating. The modern text can explain what is being said if Shakespeare's language is particularly complex or his expression antiquated. The Shakespeare text will show the reader of the modern paraphrase how much more can be expressed in poetry than in prose.

The use of *Shakespeare Made Easy* means that the newcomer need never be overcome by textual difficulties. From first to last, a measure of understanding is at hand – the key is provided for what has been a locked door to many students in the past. And as understanding grows, so an awareness develops of the potential of language as a vehicle for philosophic and moral expression, beauty and the abidingly memorable.

Even professional Shakespearean scholars can never hope to arrive at a complete understanding of the plays. Each critic, researcher, actor or producer merely adds a little to the work that has already been done, or makes fresh interpretations of the texts for new generations. For everyone, Shakespearean appreciation is a journey. *Shakespeare Made Easy* is intended to help with the first steps.

William Shakespeare

His life

William Shakespeare was born in Stratford-on-Avon, Warwickshire, on April 23, 1564, the son of a prosperous wool and leather merchant. Very little is known of his early life. From parish records we know that he married Ann Hathaway in 1582, when he was eighteen and she was twenty-six. They had three children, the eldest of whom died in childhood.

Between his marriage and the next thing we know about him, there is a gap of ten years. Probably he became a member of a traveling company of actors. By 1592 he had settled in London and had earned a reputation as an actor and playwright.

Theaters were then in their infancy. The first (called *The Theatre*) was built in 1576. Two more followed as the taste for theater grew: *The Curtain* in 1577 and *The Rose* in 1587. The demand for new plays naturally increased. Shakespeare probably earned a living adapting old plays and working in collaboration with others on new ones. Today we would call him a "freelance," since he was not permanently attached to one theater.

In 1594, a new company of actors, The Lord Chamberlain's Men, was formed, and Shakespeare was one of the shareholders. He remained a member throughout his working life. The company regrouped in 1603 and was renamed The King's Men, with James I as its patron.

Shakespeare and his fellow-actors prospered. In 1598 they built their own theater, *The Globe*, which broke away from the traditional rectangular shape of the inn and its yard (the early home of traveling bands of actors). Shakespeare described it in *Henry V* as "this wooden O," because it was circular.

Many other theaters were built by investors eager to profit from the new enthusiasm for drama. *The Hope*, *The Fortune*,

The Red Bull and *The Swan* were all open-air "public" theaters. There were also many "private" (or indoor) theaters, one of which (*The Blackfriars*) was purchased by Shakespeare and his friends because the child actors who performed there were dangerous competitors. (Shakespeare denounces them in *Hamlet*.)

After writing some thirty-seven plays (the exact number is something which scholars argue about), Shakespeare retired to his native Stratford, wealthy and respected. He died on his birthday, in 1616.

His plays

Shakespeare's plays were not all published in his lifetime. None of them comes to us exactly as he wrote it.

In Elizabethan times, plays were not regarded as either literature or good reading matter. They were written at speed (often by more than one writer), performed perhaps ten or twelve times and then discarded. Fourteen of Shakespeare's plays were first printed in Quarto (17cm × 21cm) volumes, not all with his name as the author. Some were authorized (the "good" Quartos) and probably were printed from prompt copies provided by the theater. Others were pirated (the "bad" Quartos) by booksellers who may have employed shorthand writers or bought actors' copies after the run of the play had ended.

In 1623, seven years after Shakespeare's death, John Hemming and Henry Condell (fellow-actors and shareholders in The King's Men) published a collected edition of Shakespeare's works – thirty-six plays in all – in a Folio (21cm × 34cm) edition. From their introduction it would seem that they used Shakespeare's original manuscripts ("we have scarce received from him a blot in his papers") but the Folio volumes that still survive are not all exactly alike, nor are the plays printed as we know them today, with act and scene divisions and stage directions.

A modern edition of a Shakespeare play is the result of a great deal of scholarly research and editorial skill over several centuries. The aim is always to publish a text (based on the good and bad Quartos and the Folio editions) that most closely resembles what Shakespeare intended. Misprints have added to the problems, so some words and lines are pure guesswork. This explains why some versions of Shakespeare's plays differ from others.

His theater

The first playhouse built as such in Elizabethan London, constructed in 1576, was *The Theatre*. Its co-founders were John Brayne, an investor, and James Burbage, a carpenter turned actor. Like the six or seven "public" (or outdoor) theaters which followed it over the next thirty years, it was situated outside the city, to avoid conflict with the authorities. They disapproved of players and playgoing, partly on moral and political grounds, and partly because of the danger of spreading the plague. (There were two major epidemics during Shakespeare's lifetime, and on each occasion the theaters were closed for lengthy periods.)

The Theatre was a financial success, and Shakespeare's company performed there until 1598, when a dispute over the lease of the land forced Burbage to take down the building. It was re-created in Southwark, as *The Globe*, with Shakespeare and several of his fellow-actors as the principal shareholders.

By modern standards, *The Globe* was small. Externally, the octagonal building measured less than thirty meters across, but in spite of this it could accommodate an audience of between two and three thousand people. (The largest of the three theaters at the National Theatre complex in London today seats 1160.)

Performances were advertised by means of playbills posted around the city, and they took place during the hours of daylight when the weather was suitable. A flag flew to show that all was well, to save playgoers a wasted journey.

At the entrance, a doorkeeper collected one penny (about

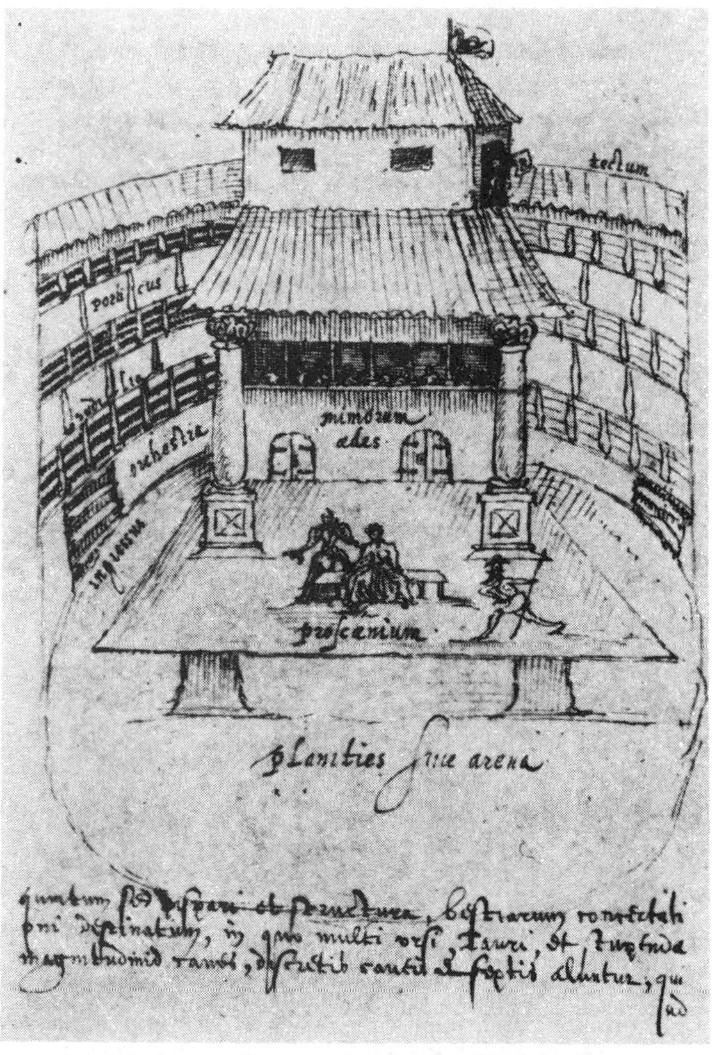

Interior of the Swan Theatre – from a pen and ink drawing made in 1596 (Mansell Collection)

60 cents today) for admission to the "pit"—a name taken from the old inn-yards, where bear-baiting and cock-fighting were popular sports. This was the minimum charge for seeing a play. The "groundlings," as they were called, simply stood around the three sides of the stage, in the open air. Those who were better off could pay extra for a seat under cover. Stairs led from the pit to three tiers of galleries around the walls. The higher one went, the more one paid. The best seats cost one shilling (or $7 today). In theaters owned by speculators like Francis Langley and Philip Henslowe, half the gallery takings went to the landlord.

A full house might consist of 800 groundlings and 1500 in the galleries, with a dozen more exclusive seats on the stage itself for the gentry. A new play might run for between six and sixteen performances; the average was about ten. As there were no breaks between scenes, and no intervals, most plays could be performed in two hours. A trumpet sounded three times before the play began.

The acting company assembled in the Tiring House at the rear of the stage. This was where they attired (or dressed) themselves: not in costumes representing the period of the play, but in Elizabethan doublet and hose. All performances were therefore in modern dress, though no expense was spared to make the stage costumes lavish. The entire company was male. By law actresses were not allowed, and female roles were performed by boys.

Access to the stage from the Tiring House was through two doors, one on each side of the stage. Because there was no front curtain, every entrance had to have its corresponding exit, so an actor killed on stage had to be carried off. There was no scenery: the audience used its imagination, guided by the spoken word. Storms and night scenes might well be performed on sunny days in mid-afternoon; the Elizabethan playgoer relied entirely on the playwright's descriptive skills to establish the dramatic atmosphere.

Once on stage, the actors and their expensive clothes were protected from sudden showers by a canopy, the underside of which was painted blue and spangled with stars to represent the heavens. A trapdoor in the stage made ghostly entrances and the gravedigging scene in *Hamlet* possible. Behind the main stage, in between the two entrance doors, there was a curtained area, concealing a small inner stage, useful for bedroom scenes. Above this was a balcony, which served for castle walls (as in *Henry V*) or a domestic balcony (as in the famous scene in *Romeo and Juliet*).

The acting style in Elizabethan times was probably more declamatory than we favor today, but the close proximity of the audience also made a degree of intimacy possible. In those days soliloquies and asides seemed quite natural. Act and scene divisions did not exist (those in printed versions of the play today have been added by editors), but Shakespeare often indicates a scene ending by a rhyming couplet.

A company such as The King's Men at *The Globe* would consist of around twenty-five actors, half of whom might be shareholders, and the rest part-timers engaged for a particular play. Among the shareholders in *The Globe* were several specialists – William Kempe, for example, was a renowned comedian and Robert Armin was a singer and dancer. Playwrights wrote parts to suit the actors who were available, and devised ways of overcoming the absence of women. Shakespeare often has his heroines dress as young men, and physical contact between lovers was formal compared with the realism we expect today.

His verse

Shakespeare wrote his plays mostly in blank verse: that is, unrhymed lines consisting of ten syllables, alternately stressed and unstressed. The technical term for this form is the iambic pentameter. When Shakespeare first began to write for the stage, it was fashionable to maintain this regular beat from the first line of the play till the last.

Shakespeare conformed at first and then experimented. Some of his early plays contain whole scenes in rhyming couplets – in *Romeo and Juliet*, for example, there is extensive use of rhyme, and as if to show his versatility, Shakespeare even inserts a sonnet into the dialog.

But as he matured, he sought greater freedom of expression than rhyme allowed. Rhyme is still used to indicate a scene ending, or to stress lines which he wishes the audience to remember. Generally, though, Shakespeare moved toward the rhythms of everyday speech. This gave him many dramatic advantages, which he fully and subtly exploits in terms of atmosphere, character, emotion, stress and pace.

It is Shakespeare's poetic imagery, however, that most distinguishes his verse from that of lesser playwrights. It enables him to stretch the imagination, express complex thought-patterns in memorable language and convey a number of associated ideas in a compressed and economical form. A study of Shakespeare's imagery – especially in his later plays – is often the key to a full understanding of his meaning and purposes.

At the other extreme is prose. Shakespeare normally reserves it for servants, clowns, commoners and pedestrian matters such as lists, messages and letters.

The Tempest

Date

The first recorded performance of *The Tempest* was in 1611, when The King's Men presented it at Court. In February 1613, the play was one of a number chosen to be part of the celebrations in honor of the marriage between James I's daughter, Elizabeth, and the Elector of Palatine. It is not known whether the texts used were identical. There is considerable evidence to support the theory that changes were made to make the play more suitable for a wedding. Some scholars think that the masque in *Act IV Scene 1* was added, and that the play was shortened elsewhere to make room for it. This could explain Prospero's lengthy exposition in *Act I Scene 2*: it might well be a summary of several scenes that had to be deleted. However, all the many theories about cuts and additions are purely speculative.

Source

No one source has been traced for the plot of *The Tempest*. The origins of some of the characters and episodes are traceable to a variety of works which would have formed part of Shakespeare's general readings. Some Italian comedies of the period have similar features; a German play has many parallels; several Spanish stories are remarkably similar; a number of history and travel books – particularly one describing a shipwreck in the Bermudas – have revealed coincidences in expression. Echoes of two passages from Montaigne's essays have been identified. It is possible that Shakespeare reworked a lost play, or dramatized a story which has not survived in print, but more probably he wrote the play as an original piece, his inspiration having the benefit of a well-read person's range and sensibility.

Text

The Tempest is the first play in the Folio Edition of 1623, and it seems to have been given particularly careful editorial treatment. There are, unusually, detailed stage directions, and the play is divided into acts and scenes. The locality is indicated - "An uninhabited island" - and a cast list is provided.

The Tempest

Original text and modern version

The characters

Alonso the king of Naples
Sebastian his brother
Prospero the rightful duke of Milan
Antonio his brother, the usurping duke of Milan
Ferdinand the son of the king of Naples
Gonzalo an honest old counsellor
Adrian, **Francisco** } lords
Caliban a deformed slave
Trinculo a jester
Stephano a drunken butler
Captain of a ship
Boatswain
Sailors
Miranda Prospero's daughter
Ariel an airy spirit
Iris, **Ceres**, **Juno**, **Nymphs**, **Reapers** } spirits

Act one

Scene 1

A ship at sea: a tempestuous noise of thunder and lightning is heard

[*Enter a* **Ship-master** *and a* **Boatswain**]

Master Boatswain!

Boatswain Here, master; what cheer?

Master Good, speak to the mariners; fall to 't, yarely, or we run ourselves aground; bestir, bestir.

[*Exit*]

[*Enter* **Mariners**]

Boatswain Heigh, my hearts! Cheerly, cheerly, my hearts! Yare, yare! Take in the topsail. Tend to th' master's whistle. Blow till thou burst thy wind, if room enough!

[*Enter* **Alonso, Sebastian, Antonio, Ferdinand, Gonzalo,** *and others*]

Alonso Good boatswain, have care. Where's the master? Play the men.

Boatswain I pray now, keep below.

Antonio Where is the master, boatswain?

Boatswain Do you not hear him? You mar our labour; keep your cabins; you do assist the storm.

Act one

Scene 1

On board a ship during a storm. A **Captain** *enters and addresses the* **Bosun**.

Captain Bosun!

Bosun [*saluting*] Aye, aye, sir. How goes it?

Captain Pipe all hands! Be quick about it, or we'll run ourselves aground. Hurry, hurry!

[*He dashes off, blowing his whistle*]

[*Sailors run on and haul at the ropes*]

Bosun Heave ho, my hearties! Put your backs into it, lads! Smartly now – take in the topsail. Obey the skipper's whistle! [*Defiantly, to the storm*] You can blow till your lungs burst, provided we've got room to maneuver!

[**Alonso** (*king of Naples*) *enters, together with* **Sebastian** (*his brother*), **Ferdinand** (*his son*), **Antonio** (*currently* **duke of Milan**), **Gonzalo** (*an elderly counsellor of state*), *and other passengers*]

Alonso Bosun, my good fellow – safety first! Where's the captain? Don't let the men give up!

Bosun Do me a favor: stay below!

Antonio Where's the captain, bosun?

Bosun Can't you hear him? [*The* **Captain** *is whistling his orders from the bridge*] You're in the way. Keep to your cabins. You're helping the storm.

Gonzalo Nay, good, be patient.

Boatswain When the sea is. Hence! What cares these roarers for the name of King? To cabin: silence! Trouble us not.

Gonzalo Good, yet remember whom thou hast aboard.

Boatswain None that I more love than myself. You are a counsellor; if you can command these elements to silence, and work the peace of the present, we will not hand a rope more; use your authority; if you cannot, give thanks you have lived so long, and make yourself ready in your cabin for the mischance of the hour, if it so hap. Cheerly, good hearts! Out of our way, I say.

[*Exit*]

Gonzalo I have great comfort from this fellow; methinks he hath no drowning mark upon him; his complexion is perfect gallows. Stand fast, good Fate, to his hanging. Make the rope of his destiny our cable, for our own doth little advantage. If he be not born to be hanged, our case is miserable.

[*Exeunt*]

[*Enter* **Boatswain**]

Boatswain Down with the topmast! yare! lower, lower! Bring her to try with main-course. [*A cry within*] A plague upon this howling! They are louder than the weather or our office.

[*Enter* **Sebastian, Antonio** *and* **Gonzalo**]

Yet again! What do you here? Shall we give o'er, and drown? Have you a mind to sink?

Sebastian A pox o' your throat, you bawling, blasphemous, incharitable dog!

Gonzalo Be patient, dear fellow . . .

Bosun When the sea is! Go! [*Pointing to the mountainous waves*] What do these roarers care about kings? Go to your cabin! Shut up, and don't get in our way!

Gonzalo Dear fellow, do remember whom you have on board . . .

Bosun Nobody I love better than myself. You're a counsellor: if you can command the elements to be silent and make these seas keep the peace, we'll not bother to haul another rope! Use your authority: if you can't, be grateful you've lived so long, and prepare yourself in your cabin for a nasty accident, in case one should happen! [*To the* **Passengers**] Get out of our way, I tell you!

[*He hurries off*]

Gonzalo This fellow gives me great comfort: he wasn't born to be drowned. He's a gallows man by the looks of him. Fate: stick to having him hanged! Make the rope that he's destined for into our anchor cable: our own is doing us no good. If he wasn't born to be hanged, we're in trouble!

[*They all go*]

[*The* **Bosun** *returns*]

Bosun [*to the* **Sailors**] Down with the topmast! Quick! Lower, lower! Let her lie hove-to with the mainsail! [*There are shouts from the* **Passengers** *below decks*] Blast all this howling! They're making more noise than the storm or us working!

[**Sebastian, Antonio** *and* **Gonzalo** *reappear*]

You again? What are you doing here? Shall we give up and drown? Do you want us to sink?

Sebastian May you choke, you bawling, blasphemous, uncharitable dog!

Boatswain Work you then?

Antonio Hang, cur! hang, you whoreson, insolent noise-maker. We are less afraid to be drowned than thou art.

Gonzalo I'll warrant him for drowning, though the ship were no stronger than a nutshell, and as leaky as an unstanched wench.

Boatswain Lay her a-hold, a-hold! set her two courses; off to sea again; lay her off.

[*Enter* **Mariners,** *wet*]

Mariners All lost, to prayers, to prayers! All lost!

[Exeunt]

Boatswain What, must our mouths be cold?

Gonzalo The King and Prince at prayers, let's assist them,
For our case is as theirs.

Sebastian I'm out of patience.

Antonio We are merely cheated of our lives by drunkards:
This wide-chapped rascal – would thou mightst lie drowning
The washing of ten tides!

Gonzalo He'll be hanged yet,
Though every drop of water swear against it,
And gape at widest to glut him.

[*A confused noise within*] 'Mercy on us!' – 'We split, we split!' – 'Farewell, my wife and children!' – 'Farewell, brother!' – 'We split, we split, we split!'

Bosun Do some work then!

Antonio Hang, you dog! Hang, you lousy, insolent loudmouth! We're less afraid of drowning than you are!

Gonzalo I guarantee he won't drown – not even if the ship's no stronger than a nutshell, and as leaky as an incontinent wench . . .

Bosun [*shouting to the* **Sailors**] Heave ho! Heave ho! Raise the mainsail and foresail! Out to sea again! Turn her around!

[**Sailors** *enter, soaking wet and in a state of panic*]

Sailors It's no good! On your knees! On your knees! It's hopeless!

[*They go*]

Bosun So it's cold mouths for us, is it? [*He takes a drink from a bottle, as sailors used to do before abandoning ship, and passes it around the crew*]

Gonzalo The king and the prince are at prayers. Let's join them. We're all in the same predicament.

Sebastian [*Watching the sailors as they drink*] This is more than I can stand!

Antonio We're cheated of our lives by drunkards! This fat-faced rascal [*he points toward the* **Bosun**] – may your drowning stretch over ten tides! [*Pirates hanged on the shoreline stayed on the gallows for only three*]

Gonzalo He'll be hanged one day, though every drop of water suggests the opposite, and the sea does its best to gulp him down!

[*A hubbub is heard: cries of "Mercy on us!" – "We're splitting up!" – "Good-bye, my wife and children!" – "Good-bye, brother!" – "We're splitting up, splitting up, splitting up!"*]

Antonio Let's all sink wi' th' King.

Sebastian Let's take leave of him.

[*Exeunt* **Antonio** *and* **Sebastian**]

Gonzalo Now would I give a thousand furlongs of sea for an acre of barren ground, long heath, broom, furze, anything. The wills above be done! But I would fain die a dry death.

[*Exeunt*]

Scene 2

The Island. Before Prospero's Cell. Enter **Prospero** *and* **Miranda**

Miranda If by your art, my dearest father, you have
Put the wild waters in this roar, allay them.
The sky, it seems, would pour down stinking pitch,
But that the sea, mounting to th' welkin's cheek,
Dashes the fire out. O, I have suffered
With those that I saw suffer! A brave vessel,
Who had, no doubt, some noble creature in her,
Dashed all to pieces. O, the cry did knock
Against my very heart! Poor souls, they perished!
Had I been any god of power, I would
Have sunk the sea within the earth, or ere
It should the good ship so have swallowed, and
The fraughting souls within her.

Antonio Let's all go down with the king.

Sebastian Let's say farewell to him.

[**Antonio** *and* **Sebastian** *leave*]

Gonzalo Just now I'd exchange a hundred miles of sea for one acre of barren ground – heath, plants – anything! God's will be done, but I'd prefer to die a dry death . . .

[*He goes*]

Scene 2

An island. A cleared space before Prospero's cave. **Prospero** *enters followed by his daughter,* **Miranda**.

Miranda Father dear: if you have raised this storm at sea by your magic, let it now subside! The sky seems to be pouring down stinking pitch, which the sea rises up to extinguish. Oh, I've suffered in sympathy with those I saw suffer! A fine ship, which no doubt had some noble people on board, was dashed to pieces. Oh, the sounds broke my heart! Poor souls, they perished! If I'd been a god with any power, I'd have made the sea disappear into the earth rather than let it swallow up that good ship and the cargo of souls aboard her!

Prospero Be collected;
No more amazement: tell your piteous heart
There's no harm done.

Miranda O, woe the day!

Prospero No harm.
I have done nothing but in care of thee,
Of thee, my dear one; thee, my daughter, who
Art ignorant of what thou art; nought knowing
Of whence I am, nor that I am more better
Than Prospero, master of a full poor cell,
And thy no greater father.

Miranda More to know
Did never meddle with my thoughts.

Prospero 'Tis time
I should inform thee farther. Lend thy hand,
And pluck my magic garment from me. So:

[*Lays down his mantle*]

Lie there, my Art. Wipe thou thine eyes; have comfort.
The direful spectacle of the wrack, which touched
The very virtue of compassion in thee,
I have with such provision in mine Art
So safely ordered, that there is no soul –
No, not so much perdition as an hair –
Betid to any creature in the vessel
Which thou heard'st cry, which thou saw'st sink. Sit down;
For thou must now know farther.

Miranda You have often
Begun to tell me what I am, but stopped,
And left me to a bootless inquisition,
Concluding, 'Stay; not yet'.

Prospero Pull yourself together. Don't be so upset. Tell your tender heart there's no harm done.

Miranda Oh, that this could happen!

Prospero There's been no harm. I've only done what's best for you, my dearest: you, my daughter, who doesn't know who she is, nor where I came from, nor that I'm something better than just Prospero, the occupier of a humble cave, and your equally humble father.

Miranda It never occurred to me to want to know more.

Prospero It's time I informed you further. Lend me a hand to remove my magic cloak. [*She does so, and he places it on a rock*] Lie there, symbol of my art! [*To* **Miranda**] Wipe your eyes. Take comfort. The dreadful business of the wreck, which touched the springs of pity in you, I've arranged so safely in accordance with my skill that not one soul is lost; nor has so much as a hair been hurt of any creature aboard whom you heard cry or saw sink beneath the waves. Sit down. Now you must know more.

Miranda You have often begun to tell me who I am, but stopped and left my questions unanswered, concluding, "No more: not yet."

Prospero The hour's now come;
The very minute bids thee ope thine ear;
Obey, and be attentive. Canst thou remember
A time before we came unto this cell?
I do not think thou canst, for then thou wast not
Out three years old.

Miranda Certainly, sir, I can.

Prospero By what? By any other house or person?
Of anything the image tell me, that
Hath kept with thy remembrance.

Miranda 'Tis far off,
And rather like a dream than an assurance
That my remembrance warrants. Had I not
Four or five women once that tended me?

Prospero Thou hadst, and more, Miranda. But how is it
That this lives in thy mind? What seest thou else
In the dark backward and abysm of time?
If thou rememb'rest aught ere thou cam'st here,
How thou cam'st here thou mayst.

Miranda But that I do not.

Prospero Twelve year since, Miranda, twelve year since,
Thy father was the Duke of Milan, and
A prince of power.

Miranda Sir, are not you my father?

Prospero Thy mother was a piece of virtue, and
She said thou wast my daughter; and thy father
Was Duke of Milan; and his only heir
And princess, no worse issued.

Miranda O the heavens!
What foul play had we, that we came from thence?
Or blessed was't we did?

Prospero The hour has now come. The time is ripe for you to hear. Do as you are told, and listen carefully. Can you remember a time before we came to this cave? I don't think you can, because then you weren't quite three years old.

Miranda Certainly, sir, I can.

Prospero What can you remember? Some other house or person? Tell me what you can recall.

Miranda It's vague and more like a dream than a definite memory. Didn't I have four or five women to look after me?

Prospero You did, and more, Miranda. What made this stick in your mind? What else can you see in the dim and distant past? If you can remember things *before* you came here, *how* you came here might come back to you.

Miranda But I can't.

Prospero Twelve years ago, Miranda, twelve years ago, your father was the duke of Milan, and a powerful prince.

Miranda Sir, are you not my father?

Prospero Your mother was chaste in the extreme, and she said you were my daughter. And I, your father, *was* duke of Milan. My only heir was a princess, equally noble in rank.

Miranda Oh God! What foul play did we suffer that caused us to leave? Or was it a good thing that we did?

Prospero Both, both, my girl;
By foul play, as thou say'st, were we heaved thence,
But blessedly holp hither.

Miranda O, my heart bleeds
To think o' th' teen that I have turned you to,
Which is from my remembrance! Please you, farther.

Prospero My brother, and thy uncle, called Antonio –
I pray thee, mark me, that a brother should
Be so perfidious! – he whom next thyself
Of all the world I loved, and to him put
The manage of my state; as at that time
Through all the signories it was the first,
And Prospero the prime duke, being so reputed
In dignity, and for the liberal Arts
Without a parallel; those being all my study,
The government I cast upon my brother,
And to my state grew stranger, being transported
And rapt in secret studies. Thy false uncle –
Dost thou attend me?

Miranda Sir, most heedfully.

Prospero Being once perfected how to grant suits,
How to deny them, who t'advance, and who
To trash for over-topping, new created
The creatures that were mine, I say, or changed 'em,
Or else new formed 'em; having both the key
Of officer and office, set all hearts i' th' state
To what tune pleased his ear; that now he was
The ivy which had hid my princely trunk,
And sucked my verdure out on't. Thou attend'st not?

Miranda O, good sir, I do.

Prospero I pray thee, mark me.
I, thus neglecting worldly ends, all dedicated

Prospero Both, both, my girl. We were ejected by foul play, as you said. But we were helped here by Divine Providence.

Miranda Oh, my heart bleeds to think of the trouble I must have been to you, which I can't remember. But please, tell me more.

Prospero My brother – your uncle – was called Antonio. Note this: that a brother should be so wicked! Next to yourself, I loved him more than anyone else in the world, and I entrusted him with the management of my kingdom. At that time, Milan was the leading state, and I was the ruling duke, because of my eminence and my unequaled understanding of the liberal arts. As this was my obsession, I left the business of government to my brother and became a stranger to my own court, being carried away and engrossed in my secret studies. Your deceitful uncle – [*he breaks off*] Are you listening to me?

Miranda Sir, most attentively.

Prospero – once he'd learned how to grant favors and how to refuse them, who to promote and who to cut down to size – won over my supporters, or replaced them, or changed their allegiance. Having both personal power and control of officials, he could call the tune in my kingdom. He'd become the parasitic ivy that hid my princely status from view and drained away my power. You're not listening!

Miranda Oh sir, I am!

Prospero Take careful note. Being dedicated to study and the

To closeness and the bettering of my mind
With that which, but by being so retired,
O'er-prized all popular rate, in my false brother
Awaked an evil nature; and my trust,
Like a good parent, did beget of him
A falsehood in its contrary, as great
As my trust was; which had indeed no limit,
A confidence sans bound. He being thus lorded,
Not only with what my revenue yielded,
But what my power might else exact, like one
Who having into truth, by telling of it,
Made such a sinner of his memory,
To credit his own lie, he did believe
He was indeed the duke; out o' th' substitution,
And executing th' outward face of royalty,
With all prerogative – hence his ambition growing –
Dost thou hear?

Miranda Your tale, sir, would cure deafness.

Prospero To have no screen between this part he played
And him he played it for, he needs will be
Absolute Milan. Me, poor man, my library
Was dukedom large enough; of temporal royalties
He thinks me now incapable; confederates,
So dry he was for sway, wi' th' King of Naples
To give him annual tribute, do him homage,
Subject his coronet to his crown, and bend
The dukedom, yet unbowed – alas, poor Milan! –
To most ignoble stooping.

Miranda O the heavens!

Prospero Mark his condition, and th' event; then tell me
If this might be a brother.

improvement of my mind with things more valuable than popular esteem, in my seclusion I neglected worldly matters. This brought out the evil side of my false brother's character. My trust, which had no limits – my confidence was absolute – generated an equal and opposite deceit in him: as when a good parent has a wicked child. Being ennobled in this way, and made rich with my income (plus what my power enabled him to extort), he began to think – like a man who believes his own lies – that he was indeed the duke, because we'd switched places, and he was carrying out my royal duties, with all the corresponding privileges. He therefore grew ambitious – Do you hear what I say?

Miranda Your story, sir, would cure deafness.

Prospero – and aspired to be the *real* duke of Milan, so there'd be no difference between the impersonator and the one for whom he was standing in. As for me, poor man, my library was all the dukedom I required. He now believes me to be incapable of handling worldly affairs. He allies himself with the king of Naples, so eager is he for power. He agrees to pay him annual protection money, to defer to his leadership, to surrender his autonomy, and subject the dukedom, hitherto proudly independent – alas, poor Milan! – to ignoble humiliation.

Miranda Oh, in the name of heaven!

Prospero Note the terms of the treaty and its results; then tell me if he was any kind of brother . . .

Miranda I should sin
To think but nobly of my grandmother:
Good wombs have borne bad sons.

Prospero Now the condition.
This King of Naples, being an enemy
To me inveterate, hearkens my brother's suit;
Which was, that he, in lieu o' th' premises
Of homage and I know not how much tribute,
Should presently extirpate me and mine
Out of the dukedom, and confer fair Milan,
With all the honours, on my brother: whereon,
A treacherous army levied, one midnight
Fated to th' purpose, did Antonio open
The gates of Milan; and, i' th' dead of darkness,
The ministers for th' purpose hurried thence
Me and thy crying self.

Miranda Alack, for pity!
I, not rememb'ring how I cried out then,
Will cry it o'er again: it is a hint
That wrings mine eyes to't.

Prospero Hear a little further,
And then I'll bring thee to the present business
Which now's upon us; without the which, this story
Were most impertinent.

Miranda Wherefore did they not
That hour destroy us?

Prospero Well demanded, wench:
My tale provokes that question. Dear, they durst not,
So dear the love my people bore me; nor set
A mark so bloody on the business; but
With colours fairer painted their foul ends.
In few, they hurried us aboard a bark,

Miranda I'd be wrong to chide my grandmother: good mothers *have* given birth to bad sons.

Prospero Now the treaty. This king of Naples, being a long-standing enemy of mine, listens to my brother's proposal. It was that in return for homage and I don't know how much tribute money, he should instantly expel me and my family from the dukedom and confer the title on my brother. Thereupon, a treacherous army was raised, and one fatal midnight Antonio opened the gates of Milan. At the dead of night his henchmen hurried us through – me, and you in tears.

Miranda Alas, for pity's sake! Not remembering how I cried then, I'll weep over it now. It brings tears to my eyes.

Prospero Hear a little more. Then I'll bring you to the latest development, without which this story would be quite irrelevant.

Miranda Why didn't they kill us then?

Prospero A good question, my girl. My narrative prompts it. Dear, they didn't dare. My people loved me too much, and they didn't want the business to be stained with blood. They painted a prettier picture of their foul purposes. In short, they hurried us aboard a ship and took us several miles out to sea. There they'd prepared a rotten carcass of a hulk,

Bore us some leagues to sea; where they prepared
A rotten carcass of a butt, not rigged,
Nor tackle, sail, nor mast; the very rats
Instinctively have quit it: there they hoist us,
To cry to th' sea that roared to us; to sigh
To th' winds, whose pity, sighing back again,
Did us but loving wrong.

Miranda Alack, what trouble
Was I then to you!

Prospero O, a cherubim
Thou wast that did preserve me. Thou didst smile,
Infused with a fortitude from heaven,
When I have decked the sea with drops full salt,
Under my burthen groaned; which raised in me
An undergoing stomach, to bear up
Against what should ensue.

Miranda How came we ashore?

Prospero By Providence divine.
Some food we had, and some fresh water, that
A noble Neapolitan, Gonzalo,
Out of his charity, who being then appointed
Master of this design, did give us, with
Rich garments, linens, stuffs and necessaries,
Which since have steaded much; so, of his gentleness,
Knowing I loved my books, he furnished me
From mine own library with volumes that
I prize above my dukedom.

Miranda Would I might
But ever see that man!

Prospero Now I arise;
Sit still, and hear the last of our sea-sorrow.
Here in this island we arrived; and here
Have I, thy schoolmaster, made thee more profit

with neither rigging, nor tackle, nor sails, nor mast. Even the rats had instinctively left it. To this they transferred us, to cry to the sea that roared at us, to sigh to the winds that only made things worse by sighing back.

Miranda Alas, what a trouble I was to you then!

Prospero Oh, you were a little angel who saved me. You smiled, divinely courageous, when I sprinkled the sea with salty tears, and groaned under my misfortunes. This gave me the stomach to endure what might happen later.

Miranda How did we reach shore?

Prospero By Divine Providence. We had some food and some fresh water, given us by Gonzalo, a noble Neapolitan in charge of the operation, along with fine clothes, linens, materials and essentials which have since stood us in good stead. And out of the kindness of his heart, knowing I loved my books, he provided me with volumes from my own library that I valued more than my dukedom.

Miranda I hope I might see that man some day!

Prospero Things now get better for me. Sit still, and hear the end of our troubles at sea. We arrived here on this island, and here, as your schoolmaster, I've given you an education

Than other princess' can, that have more time
For vainer hours, and tutors not so careful.

Miranda Heavens thank you for't! And now, I pray you, sir,
For still 'tis beating in my mind, your reason
For raising this sea-storm?

Prospero Know thus far forth.
By accident most strange, bountiful Fortune,
Now my dear lady, hath mine enemies
Brought to this shore; and by my prescience
I find my zenith doth depend upon
A most auspicious star, whose influence
If now I court not, but omit, my fortunes
Will ever after droop. Here cease more questions.
Thou art inclined to sleep; 'tis a good dulness,
And give it way: I know thou canst not choose.

[**Miranda** *sleeps*]

Come away, servant, come. I am ready now.
Approach, my Ariel, come.

[*Enter* **Ariel**]

Ariel All hail, great master! Grave sir, hail! I come
To answer thy best pleasure; be 't to fly,
To swim, to dive into the fire, to ride
On the curled clouds, to thy strong bidding task
Ariel and all his quality.

Prospero Hast thou, spirit,
Performed to point the tempest that I bade thee?

Ariel To every article.
I boarded the king's ship; now on the beak,
Now in the waist, the deck, in every cabin,
I flamed amazement; sometime I'd divide,

better than that of other princesses who have more time for trivialities, and whose tutors aren't so dedicated.

Miranda Heaven be thanked! And now, please, sir – because I can't get it out of my mind – what is your reason for raising this storm at sea?

Prospero I'll tell you this much for now. By a curious coincidence, benevolent Fortune (now running in my favor) has brought my enemies to this shore. My gift of second sight tells me that this is my great opportunity. If I don't grasp it now, my prospects can only get worse. Ask no more questions. [*He passes his hand across her eyes*] You feel sleepy. It's a benign drowsiness. Give in to it. I know you have no choice.

[**Miranda** *falls asleep, as if hypnotized.* **Prospero** *calls softly*]

Come here, servant. Come! I am ready now. Approach, my Ariel, come!

[**Ariel**, *a spirit, enters*]

Ariel All hail, great master! Learned sir, hail! I come to do your bidding, whether it be to fly, to swim, to dive into fire, to ride on the billowy clouds. Ariel and all his fellow spirits are at your command.

Prospero Spirit: have you fully enacted the tempest that I ordered?

Ariel In every detail. I boarded the king's ship. At the prow, amidships, on the deck, in every cabin – as a fireball I struck terror. Sometimes I'd split up, and burn in several places;

And burn in many places; on the topmast,
The yards and bowsprit, would I flame distinctly,
Then meet and join. Jove's lightnings, the precursors
O' th' dreadful thunder-claps, more momentary
And sight-outrunning were not; the fire and cracks
Of sulphurous roaring the most mighty Neptune
Seem to besiege, and make his bold waves tremble,
Yea, his dread trident shake.

Prospero My brave spirit!
Who was so firm, so constant, that this coil
Would not infect his reason?

Ariel Not a soul
But felt a fever of the mad, and played
Some tricks of desperation. All but mariners
Plunged in the foaming brine, and quit the vessel,
Then all afire with me. The King's son, Ferdinand,
With hair up-staring – then like reeds, not hair –
Was the first man that leaped; cried, 'Hell is empty,
And all the devils are here!'

Prospero Why, that's my spirit!
But was not this nigh shore?

Ariel Close by, my master.

Prospero But are they, Ariel, safe?

Ariel Not a hair perished;
On their sustaining garments not a blemish,
But fresher than before; and, as thou bad'st me,
In troops I have dispersed them 'bout the isle.
The King's son have I landed by himself;
Whom I left cooling of the air with sighs
In an odd angle of the isle, and sitting,
His arms in this sad knot.

on the topmast, yardarms, and bowsprit, I'd appear as separate flames, then meet and join as one. Lightning flashes, which precede fearful claps of thunder, were never more sustained and numerous to see. Fire and explosive blasts seemed to besiege mighty Neptune, the sea king, making his bold waves tremble and his dreaded trident shake.

Prospero My most excellent spirit! Who could be so courageous, so resolute, that this uproar had no effect on his mind?

Ariel Everyone felt a touch of madness and behaved frantically. All except the sailors plunged into the foaming brine and abandoned ship, it being all on fire at the time with me. The king's son, Ferdinand, with his hair standing on end – it looked more like reeds than hair – was the first man to leap, crying, "Hell is empty. All the devils are here!"

Prospero Why, that's my spirit! But wasn't this near shore?

Ariel Close by, my master.

Prospero But are they safe, Ariel?

Ariel Not a hair of their heads is hurt. There's not a mark on their buoyant garments; they are fresher than before. And as you ordered, I've spread them around the island in groups. The king's son I've landed by himself; I left him sighing away in an odd corner of the island and sitting with his arms folded in misery like this. [*He demonstrates*]

Prospero Of the King's ship,
The mariners, say how thou hast disposed,
And all the rest o' th' fleet.

Ariel Safely in harbour
Is the King's ship; in the deep nook, where once
Thou call'dst me up at midnight to fetch dew
From the still-vexed Bermoothes, there she's hid:
The mariners all under hatches stowed;
Who, with a charm joined to their suffered labour,
I have left asleep; and for the rest o' th' fleet,
Which I dispersed, they all have met again,
And are upon the Mediterranean flote,
Bound sadly home for Naples;
Supposing that they saw the King's ship wracked,
And his great person perish.

Prospero Ariel, thy charge
Exactly is performed; but there's more work.
What is the time o' th' day?

Ariel Past the mid season.

Prospero At least two glasses. The time 'twixt six and now
Must by us both be spent most preciously.

Ariel Is there more toil? Since thou dost give me pains,
Let me remember thee what thou hast promised,
Which is not yet performed me.

Prospero How now? Moody?
What is't thou canst demand?

Ariel My liberty.

Prospero Before the time be out? No more!

Ariel I prithee,
Remember I have done thee worthy service;

Prospero What have you done with the king's ship, the sailors, and the rest of the fleet?

Ariel The king's ship is safely in harbor. It's hidden in the deep cove where you once called on me at midnight to fetch magic dew from the stormy Bermudas. The sailors are all stowed below decks; I've left them asleep, with a spell working in conjunction with their exhaustion. As for the rest of the fleet, which I scattered, they've all met up again and are on the Mediterranean Sea, bound for Naples in great sadness, thinking they saw the king's ship wrecked and the king himself drowned.

Prospero Ariel, you've carried out orders exactly. But there's more work. What's the time?

Ariel Past midday.

Prospero At least two o'clock. We've both got to make the most of the time between now and six tonight.

Ariel Is there more hard work? Since you are so demanding, let me remind you of what you promised, which you haven't yet granted me.

Prospero [*bridling*] What? Moody? What can *you* demand?

Ariel My freedom.

Prospero Before you've served your time? No more of that!

Ariel With respect, remember that I have served you worthily: told you no lies, made no mistakes, served without

Told thee no lies, made no mistakings, served
Without or grudge or grumblings: thou did promise
To bate me a full year.

Prospero Dost thou forget
From what a torment I did free thee?

Ariel No.

Prospero Thou dost, and think'st it much to tread the ooze
Of the salt deep,
To run upon the sharp wind of the north,
To do me business in the veins o' th' earth
When it is baked with frost.

Ariel I do not, sir.

Prospero Thou liest, malignant thing! Hast thou forgot
The foul witch Sycorax, who with age and envy
Was grown into a hoop? Hast thou forgot her?

Ariel No, sir.

Prospero Thou hast. Where was she born? Speak: tell me.

Ariel Sir, in Argier.

Prospero O, was she so? I must
Once in a month recount what thou hast been,
Which thou forget'st. This damned witch Sycorax,
For mischiefs manifold, and sorceries terrible
To enter human hearing, from Argier,
Thou know'st, was banished: for one thing she did
They would not take her life. Is not this true?

Ariel Ay, sir.

Prospero This blue-eyed hag was hither brought with child,
And here was left by th' sailors. Thou, my slave,
As thou report'st thyself, was then her servant;
And, for thou wast a spirit too delicate

grudging or grumbling. You promised to release me a year early.

Prospero Have you forgotten the torment I freed you from?

Ariel No.

Prospero You have, and now you think it's too much trouble to walk on the ocean floor, to ride on the sharp wind of the North, to do my bidding in subterranean waters, when the earth is hard with frost.

Ariel I don't, sir.

Prospero You're lying, you evil thing! Have you forgotten the foul witch Sycorax, who was bent double with old age and malice? Have you forgotten her?

Ariel No, sir.

Prospero You have! Where was she born? Speak: tell me!

Ariel Sir, in Algiers.

Prospero Oh, was she really? Once a month I must go over what you have been, which you forget. This damned witch Sycorax was banished from Algiers, as you know, for innumerable misdeeds and sorceries unfit for the human ear. They would not execute her on account of one thing. Isn't this true?

Ariel Yes, sir.

Prospero This hollow-eyed hag was brought here pregnant and left here by the sailors. You – my "slave," as you describe yourself – were her servant then. Because you were too sensitive a spirit to carry out her gross and

To act her earthy and abhorred commands,
Refusing her grand hests, she did confine thee,
By help of her more potent ministers,
And in her most unmitigable rage,
Into a cloven pine; within which rift
Imprisoned thou didst painfully remain
A dozen years; within which space she died,
And left thee there; where thou didst vent thy groans
As fast as mill-wheels strike. Then was this island –
Save for the son that she did litter here,
A freckled whelp hag-born – not honoured with
A human shape.

Ariel Yes, Caliban her son.

Prospero Dull thing I say so; he, that Caliban,
Whom now I keep in service. Thou best know'st
What torment I did find thee in; thy groans
Did make wolves howl, and penetrate the breasts
Of ever-angry bears: it was a torment
To lay upon the damned, which Sycorax
Could not again undo: it was mine Art,
When I arrived and heard thee, that made gape
The pine, and let thee out.

Ariel I thank thee, master.

Prospero If thou more murmur'st, I will rend an oak,
And peg thee in his knotty entrails, till
Thou hast howled away twelve winters.

Ariel Pardon, master:
I will be correspondent to command,
And do my spriting gently.

Prospero Do so; and after two days
I will discharge thee.

repulsive commands, in an uncontrollable rage she imprisoned you inside a split pine tree, aided by her more powerful subordinates, for refusing to obey her orders. Inside that crevice, in great pain, you remained imprisoned for twelve years. During that time she died and left you there, where you groaned as fast as mill wheels hit the water. At that time, except for the son which she gave birth to here – a freckled whelp, hag-born – there were no humans on this island.

Ariel Yes: her son Caliban.

Prospero Dunce! That's who I mean: Caliban, my servant. You know best the torment you were in when I found you. Your groans made wolves howl; they touched the hearts of hot-tempered bears. It was a torment of the damned, which Sycorax could not reverse. It was my magic art, when I arrived and heard you, that made the pine open up and let you out.

Ariel I thank you, master.

Prospero Complain again, and I'll split an oak and peg you inside its knotty innards till you've howled away twelve winters!

Ariel Pardon, master. I'll be obedient to your commands and do my duties as a spirit submissively.

Prospero Do so, and two days from now I shall release you.

Ariel That's my noble master!
What shall I do? Say what: what shall I do?

Prospero Go make thyself like a nymph o' th' sea:
But subject to
No sight but thine and mine; invisible
To every eyeball else. Go take this shape,
And hither come in't: Go, hence with diligence.

[*Exit* **Ariel**]

Awake, dear heart, awake! Thou hast slept well;
Awake!

Miranda The strangeness of your story put
Heaviness in me.

Prospero Shake it off. Come on;
We'll visit Caliban my slave, who never
Yields us kind answer.

Miranda 'Tis a villain, sir,
I do not love to look on.

Prospero But, as 'tis,
We cannot miss him; he does make our fire,
Fetch in our wood, and serves in offices
That profit us. What, ho! slave! Caliban!
Thou earth, thou! Speak!

Caliban [*Within*] There's wood enough within.

Prospero Come forth, I say! There's other business for thee;
Come, thou tortoise! When?

[*Enter* **Ariel** *like a water-nymph*]

Fine apparition! My quaint Ariel,
Hark in thine ear.

Ariel That's my noble master! What shall I do? Tell me: what shall I do?

Prospero Make yourself into a sea nymph. Be invisible to everyone but you and me. Go, take this shape, and return in it. Go, and do as I order.

[**Ariel** *goes.* **Prospero** *turns to the sleeping* **Miranda**]

Wake up, dear heart, wake up! You have slept well. Wake up!

Miranda The strangeness of your story made me drowsy.

Prospero Shake off your drowsiness. Come on, we'll visit my slave Caliban, who never answers us respectfully. [*He turns to the opening of a cave nearby*]

Miranda He's a villain, sir, I don't like to see.

Prospero As things are, we can't do without him. He lights our fire, fetches our wood, and is generally useful to us. [*Calling*] Hey there! Slave! Caliban! You clod, you! Answer!

Caliban [*inside*] There's enough wood inside.

Prospero Come out, I say! There are other jobs for you. Come here, you tortoise! How much longer?

[**Ariel** *returns, looking like a sea nymph*]

A splendid likeness! My ingenious Ariel! A word in your ear. [*He whispers*]

Ariel My lord, it shall be done.

[*Exit*]

Prospero Thou poisonous slave, got by the devil himself
Upon thy wicked dam, come forth!

[*Enter* **Caliban**]

Caliban As wicked dew as e'er my mother brushed
With raven's feather from unwholesome fen
Drop on you both! A south-west blow on ye
And blister you all o'er!

Prospero For this, be sure, to-night thou shalt have cramps,
Side-stitches that shall pen thy breath up; urchins
Shall, for that vast of night that they may work,
All exercise on thee; thou shalt be pinched
As thick as honeycomb, each pinch more stinging
Than bees that made 'em.

Caliban I must eat my dinner.
This island's mine, by Sycorax my mother,
Which thou takest from me. When thou cam'st first,
Thou strok'st me, and made much of me; wouldst give me
Water with berries in 't; and teach me how
To name the bigger light, and how the less,
That burn by day and night: and then I loved thee,
And showed thee all the qualities o' th' isle,
The fresh springs, brine-pits, barren place and fertile:
Cursed be I that did so! All the charms
Of Sycorax, toads, beetles, bats, light on you!
For I am all the subjects that you have,
Which first was mine own King; and here you sty me
In this hard rock, whiles you do keep from me
The rest o' th' island.

Ariel My lord, it shall be done.

[*He goes*]

Prospero [*to* **Caliban**] You poisonous slave, sired by the devil himself upon your wicked mother – come out!

[**Caliban**, *an ugly and deformed creature, enters*]

Caliban May as wicked a fog as ever my mother swept from a putrid bog with a raven's feather drop on you both! May a southwest pestilential wind blow on you and blister you all over!

Prospero For saying that, you'll suffer cramps tonight, for sure! Side stitches, that will cut your breath short! Goblins will get to work on you throughout the long night hours between curfew and cockcrow! You'll be pinched till your skin resembles the checkered pattern of the honeycomb, each pinch worse than a bee sting.

Caliban I have to eat my dinner! This island's mine, through my mother Sycorax, and you've taken it from me. When you first came, you stroked me and made much of me. You'd give me water with berries in it and teach me what to call the big light that burns during the day and the smaller one that shines at night. I loved you then and showed you all the features of the island: the fresh springs and the salt pits; the barren places and those that are fertile. Curse me for doing so! May all the spells of Sycorax – toads and beetles and bats – befall you! I am all the subjects you have; I, who was once my own king! You pen me in a cave and keep me away from the rest of the island.

Prospero Thou most lying slave,
Whom stripes may move, not kindness! I have used thee,
Filth as thou art, with human care; and lodged thee
In mine own cell, till thou didst seek to violate
The honour of my child.

Caliban O ho, O ho! would't had been done!
Thou didst prevent me; I had peopled else
This isle with Calibans.

Miranda Abhorred slave,
Which any print of goodness wilt not take,
Being capable of all ill! I pitied thee,
Took pains to make thee speak, taught thee each hour
One thing or other: when thou didst not, savage,
Know thine own meaning, but wouldst gabble like
A thing most brutish, I endowed thy purposes
With words that made them known. But thy vile race,
Though thou didst learn, had that in't which good natures
Could not abide to be with; therefore wast thou
Deservedly confined into this rock,
Who hadst deserved more than a prison.

Caliban You taught me language; and my profit on't
Is, I know how to curse. The red plague rid you
For learning me your language!

Prospero Hag-seed, hence!
Fetch us in fuel; and be quick, thou'rt best,
To answer other business. Shrug'st thou, malice?
If thou neglect'st, or dost unwillingly
What I command, I'll rack thee with old cramps,
Fill all thy bones with aches, make thee roar,
That beasts shall tremble at thy din.

Caliban No, pray thee.
[*Aside*] I must obey: his Art is of such power,

Prospero You lying slave, you! Whipping works with you, not kindness! Filth though you are, I've treated you humanely! I let you sleep in my own cave, till you tried to rape my daughter!

Caliban Oh ho! Oh ho! I wish I had! You stopped me. Otherwise I'd have peopled this island with Calibans!

Miranda You disgusting slave! Goodness makes no impression on you; you're all evil! I pitied you – took the trouble to teach you to speak; not an hour passed but I taught you something or other. At that time, savage, you couldn't organize your own thoughts but used to gabble like a brute; I gave you language to express yourself. But your natural disposition, in spite of education, was abhorrent to decent people. Therefore you were rightly confined to this cave, though you'd deserved more than just a prison.

Caliban You taught me language: my profit from that is, I know how to curse! May the plague with its red sores destroy you for teaching me your language!

Prospero Off with you, you son of a witch! Bring in some fuel for us, and in future you'd better be quick about your business! [**Caliban** *gestures his indifference*] Do you shrug your shoulders, you malicious object? If you disobey my orders, or work halfheartedly, I'll rack you with miserable cramps, fill your bones with aches, and make you roar so loud that beasts will tremble at your groans.

Caliban [*shrinking away in fear*] No, please don't! [*Aside*] I've got to obey. His magic is so powerful it would control

It would control my dam's god, Setebos,
And make a vassal of him.

Prospero So, slave; hence!

[*Exit* **Caliban**]

[*Enter* **Ariel**, *invisible, playing and singing;* **Ferdinand** *following*]

Ariel *Come unto these yellow sands,*
And then take hands:
Curtsied when you have and kissed
The wild waves whist:
Foot it featly here and there,
And sweet sprites bear
The burthen. Hark, hark.

[*Burthen dispersedly*] *Bow-wow.*

Ariel *The watch dogs bark:*

[*Burthen dispersedly*] *Bow-wow.*

Ariel *Hark, hark! I hear*
The strain of strutting chanticleer

Cry – [*Burthen dispersedly*] *Cock a diddle dow.*

Ferdinand Where should this music be? i' th' air or th' earth?
It sounds no more: and, sure, it waits upon
Some god o' th' island. Sitting on a bank,
Weeping again the King my father's wrack,
This music crept by me upon the waters,
Allaying both their fury and my passion
With its sweet air: thence I have followed it,
Or it hath drawn me rather. But 'tis gone.
No, it begins again.

Setebos, my mother's god, and make a servant of him.

Prospero So, slave – go!

[**Caliban** *shuffles off*]

[**Ariel** *enters; he is invisible to all but* **Prospero**. *He is singing to his own accompaniment.* **Ferdinand** *follows him*]

Ariel *Come unto these yellow sands*
And then take hands.
Curtsy next, and kiss; this will
The wild waves still.
Make the dance a graceful thing;
Sweet spirits sing
The chorus. Hark, hark . . .

Chorus *Bow-wow!*

Ariel *The watchdogs bark:*

Chorus *Bow-wow!*

Ariel *Hark, hark! I hear*
The cockcrow of proud chanticleer
Cry:

Chorus *Cock-a-doodle-do!*

Ferdinand Where is this music coming from? The air, or the earth? [*He listens carefully*] It has stopped. For sure, it's to entertain some god of the island. This music crept up on me on the seashore, as I was sitting on a bank weeping yet again for the shipwreck of my father. Its sweet melody calmed the storm and my distress. I've followed it from there: or rather, it has led me. But it's gone now. [**Ariel** *resumes his song*] Now it begins again . . .

Ariel *Full fathom five thy father lies;*
Of his bones are coral made;
Those are pearls that were his eyes:
Nothing of him that doth fade,
But doth suffer a sea-change
Into something rich and strange.
Sea-nymphs hourly ring his knell.

[*Burthen*] *Ding-dong.*

Ariel *Hark! now I hear them – Ding-dong, bell.*

Ferdinand The ditty does remember my drowned father.
This is no mortal business, nor no sound
That the earth owes: I hear it now above me.

Prospero The fringed curtains of thine eye advance,
And say what thou seest yond.

Miranda What is't? A spirit?
Lord, how it looks about! Believe me, sir,
It carries a brave form. But 'tis a spirit.

Prospero No, wench; it eats and sleeps and hath such senses
As we have, such. This gallant which thou seest
Was in the wrack; and, but he's something stained
With grief – that's beauty's canker – thou mightst call him
A goodly person; he hath lost his fellows,
And strays about to find 'em.

Miranda I might call him
A thing divine; for nothing natural
I ever saw so noble.

Prospero [*Aside*] It goes on, I see,
As my soul prompts it. Spirit, fine spirit! I'll free thee
Within two days for this.

Ferdinand Most sure the goddess
On whom these airs attend! Vouchsafe my prayer

Ariel *Five fathoms deep thy father lies;*
His bones have coral made.
Those are pearls that were his eyes:
All his parts that have decayed
The sea has changed beyond compare
Into something rich and rare.
Sea nymphs hourly toll his knell –

Chorus *Ding-dong . . .*

Ariel *Hark! Now I hear them: ding-dong, bell.*

Ferdinand The song commemorates my drowned father. This is not a natural thing, nor a sound belonging to this earth. I can hear it now, above me.

Prospero [*to* **Miranda**] Open your eyes and tell me what you see over there.

Miranda [*admiring* **Ferdinand**] What is it? A spirit? My, how it looks around! Believe me, sir, it's very handsome. But it's a spirit.

Prospero No, my girl. It eats and sleeps and has the very same senses as we have. This gentleman you see was in the shipwreck. Except for being rather tearstained (which is bad for beauty!) you could call him a good-looking person. He has lost his companions and is wandering about to find them.

Miranda I'm tempted to call him divine, since I've never seen anything on earth so noble!

Prospero [*aside*] It's turning out as I hoped. [*To* **Ariel**] Spirit, fine spirit! I'll free you within two days for this!

Ferdinand [*seeing* **Miranda** *for the first time*] This must surely be the goddess for whom this music was played. [*To* **Miranda**] May I humbly beg to know whether you live on this

May know if you remain upon this island;
And that you will some good instruction give
How I may bear me here: my prime request,
Which I do last pronounce, is, O you wonder!
If you be maid or no?

Miranda No wonder, sir;
But certainly a maid.

Ferdinand My language! Heavens!
I am the best of them that speak this speech,
Were I but where 'tis spoken.

Prospero How? the best?
What wert thou, if the King of Naples heard thee?

Ferdinand A single thing, as I am now, that wonders
To hear thee speak of Naples. He does hear me;
And that he does I weep; myself am Naples,
Who with mine eyes, never since at ebb, beheld
The King my father wracked.

Miranda Alack, for mercy!

Ferdinand Yes, faith, and all his lords; the Duke of Milan
And his brave son being twain.

Prospero [*Aside*] The Duke of Milan
And his more braver daughter could control thee,
If now 'twere fit to do't. At the first sight
They have changed eyes. Delicate Ariel,
I'll set thee free for this. [*To* **Ferdinand**] A word, good sir;
I fear you have done yourself some wrong; a word.

Miranda Why speaks my father so ungently? This
Is the third man that e'er I saw; the first
That e'er I sighed for: pity move my father
To be inclined my way!

island? Will you advise me how I should conduct myself here? And lastly, but it's really my most important question: oh, you marvel! are you a mortal young woman or not?

Miranda No marvel, sir, but I'm certainly a girl.

Ferdinand My own language! Amazing! If I were now where it's spoken, I'd be the highest in rank of those who speak it.

Prospero What, the highest? If the king of Naples heard you say that, what would you be?

Ferdinand A lonesome man, as I am now, who's surprised to hear you speak of the king. He *does* hear me. And that he does, I grieve, because *I* am the king of Naples. With my own eyes, which haven't been dry since, I saw my father the king shipwrecked.

Miranda Oh, how awful!

Ferdinand Yes indeed, and all his lords; the duke of Milan and his brave son being two of them.

Prospero [*aside*] The duke of Milan and his even braver daughter could prove you wrong if this were the right time. [*Observing* **Ferdinand** *and* **Miranda**] It is love at first sight. Delicate Ariel, I'll set you free for this! [*To* **Ferdinand**] A word, dear sir. I think you are mistaken. A word with you . . .

Miranda Why does my father speak so rudely? This is the third man I've ever seen, the first I've ever doted on. May pity move my father to see things my way!

Ferdinand O, if a virgin,
And your affection not gone forth, I'll make you
The Queen of Naples.

Prospero Soft, sir! one word more.
[*Aside*] They are both in either's powers: but this swift business
I must uneasy make, lest too light winning
Make the prize light. [*To* **Ferdinand**] One word more: I charge thee
That thou attend me: thou dost here usurp
The name thou ow'st not; and hast put thyself
Upon this island as a spy, to win it
From me, the lord on't.

Ferdinand No, as I am a man.

Miranda There's nothing ill can dwell in such a temple:
If the ill spirit have so fair a house,
Good things will strive to dwell with't.

Prospero Follow me.
Speak not you for him: he's a traitor. Come;
I'll manacle thy neck and feet together:
Sea-water shalt thou drink; thy food shall be
The fresh-brook mussels, withered roots, and husks
Wherein the acorn cradled. Follow.

Ferdinand No;
I will resist such entertainment till
Mine enemy has more power.

[*He draws, and is charmed from moving*]

Miranda O dear father,
Make not too rash a trial of him, for
He's gentle, and not fearful.

Ferdinand Oh, if you are a virgin and not committed to another, I'll make you queen of Naples!

Prospero Enough of that, sir! A word. . . . [*Aside*] They are infatuated with each other, so I must put difficulties in the way of this fast progress, in case the ease of winning undervalues the prize. [*To* **Ferdinand**] A further word: I insist you listen. You are an impostor, and you have come to this island as a spy, to take it from me, its lord!

Ferdinand No, upon my honor!

Miranda Nothing wicked could reside within such a temple! If evil were so handsomely housed, good would drive it out.

Prospero [*to* **Ferdinand**] Follow me. [*To* **Miranda**] Don't plead on his behalf: he's a traitor! [*To* **Ferdinand**] Come; I'll manacle your neck and feet together. You'll drink salt water. Your food will be freshwater mussels, shrunken roots, and acorn husks. Follow me!

Ferdinand No! I won't submit to that kind of entertainment till my enemy's more powerful! [*He draws his sword, but* **Prospero** *casts a spell on him. He cannot move*]

Miranda Oh, dear father: don't treat him too harshly. He's of noble birth and no threat to you.

Prospero What! I say,
My foot my tutor? Put thy sword up, traitor;
Who makest a show, but darest not strike, thy conscience
Is so possessed with guilt: come from thy ward;
For I can here disarm thee with this stick
And make thy weapon drop.

Miranda Beseech you, father.

Prospero Hence! Hang not on my garments.

Miranda Sir, have pity;
I'll be his surety.

Prospero Silence! One word more
Shall make me chide thee, if not hate thee. What!
And advocate for an impostor! Hush!
Thou think'st there is no more such shapes as he,
Having seen but him and Caliban: foolish wench!
To th' most of men this is a Caliban,
And they to him are angels.

Miranda My affections
Are then most humble; I have no ambition
To see a goodlier man.

Prospero Come on; obey;
Thy nerves are in their infancy again,
And have no vigour in them.

Ferdinand So they are:
My spirits, as in a dream, are all bound up.
My father's loss, the weakness which I feel,
The wrack of all my friends, nor this man's threats,
To whom I am subdued, are but light to me,
Might I but through my prison once a day
Behold this maid: all corners else o' th' earth
Let liberty make use of; space enough
Have I in such a prison.

Prospero What! Do you think my brains are in my feet? [*To* **Ferdinand**] Sheathe your sword, traitor. You go through the motions, but you have such a guilty conscience you daren't strike a blow. Drop your guard! I can disarm you with this stick – [*he flicks his magic wand, knocking* **Ferdinand***'s sword from his spellbound hand*] – and make you drop your weapon.

Miranda Father, I beg you –

Prospero [*brushing her off*] Be off! Don't pull my clothes!

Miranda Sir, have pity! I'll be his guarantor.

Prospero Silence! One more word and I must scold you, if not hate you. What? Defend an impostor? Quiet! You think there are no more of his kind, because you've seen only him and Caliban! You silly girl! *He's* a Caliban compared with most men! Compared with him, they're angels.

Miranda My tastes are very simple, then. I have no ambition to see a handsomer man.

Prospero [*To* **Ferdinand***, who is slowly recovering the use of his limbs*] Come on, do as you're told. Your muscles are as weak and helpless as a baby's.

Ferdinand So they are. My senses are all numb, as in a dream. The loss of my father, my feeling of weakness, the shipwrecking of all my friends, not to mention the threats of this man who has me in his power, are all of no consequence to me provided I can see this girl once a day from my prison. Free men can have the rest of the world: I've got all the room I want here in this jail.

Prospero [*Aside*] It works.
[*To* **Ferdinand**] Come on.
[*To* **Ariel**] Thou hast done well, fine Ariel! Follow me;
Hark what thou else shalt do me.

Miranda Be of comfort;
My father's of a better nature, sir,
Than he appears by speech: this is unwonted
Which now came from him.

Prospero Thou shalt be as free
As mountain winds: but then exactly do
All points of my command.

Ariel To th' syllable.

Prospero Come, follow. Speak not for him.

[*Exeunt*]

Prospero [*aside*] It's working. [*To* **Ferdinand**] Come on! [*To* **Ariel**] You've done well, my fine Ariel! Follow me: listen to what else you can do for me.

Miranda [*to* **Ferdinand**] Don't despair. My father's nicer than his speech suggests. His behavior now is untypical.

Prospero [*to* **Ariel**] You shall be as free as the mountain winds. But do exactly as I say.

Ariel To the last syllable.

Prospero [*to* **Ferdinand**] Come, follow me. [*To* **Miranda**] Don't plead for him!

[*They leave*]

Act two

Scene 1

Another part of the Island. Enter **Alonso, Sebastian, Antonio, Gonzalo, Adrian, Francisco,** *and others*

Gonzalo Beseech you, sir, be merry; you have cause,
So have we all, of joy; for our escape
Is much beyond our loss. Our hint of woe
Is common; every day, some sailor's wife,
The masters of some merchant, and the merchant,
Have just our theme of woe; but for the miracle,
I mean our preservation, few in millions
Can speak like us: then wisely, good sir, weigh
Our sorrow with our comfort.

Alonso Prithee, peace.

Sebastian [*Aside to* **Antonio**] He receives comfort like cold porridge.

Antonio [*Aside to* **Sebastian**] The visitor will not give him o'er so.

Sebastian [*Aside to* **Antonio**] Look, he's winding up the watch of his wit; by and by it will strike.

Gonzalo Sir –

Sebastian [*Aside to* **Antonio**] One: tell.

Gonzalo When every grief is entertained that's offered,
Comes to th' entertainer –

Sebastian A dollar.

Act two

Scene 1

Another part of the island. **Alonso, Sebastian, Antonio, Gonzalo, Adrian, Francisco**, *and the other survivors enter.*

Gonzalo [*trying to spread some comfort*] I beg you, sir, cheer up. You've good reason for joy, as we all have. What we've lost is nothing compared with our escape. The reason for our distress is common. Every day, some sailor's wife, the owners of some ship, and the trader who chartered it have exactly the same reason for sorrow as we have. As for the miracle – by which I mean our survival – few people in millions can claim our luck. So, dear sir, weigh our misery sensibly against our consolations.

Alonso Please, that's enough.

Sebastian [*aside to* **Antonio**] Comfort's like cold porridge to him.

Antonio [*to* **Sebastian**, *and sneering at* **Gonzalo**] The social worker won't give up so easily.

Sebastian [*to* **Antonio**, *agreeing*] Look, he's winding up the watch of his wit. [**Gonzalo** *is thinking hard and preparing for another speech of good cheer*] Any moment now, he'll strike!

Gonzalo [*to* **Alonso**] Sir –

Sebastian [*to* **Antonio**] One! Keep count!

Gonzalo [*wordily*] When one has entertained every possible grief, there comes to the entertainer –

Sebastian His fee. A dollar piece?

Gonzalo Dolour comes to him, indeed: you have spoken truer than you purposed.

Sebastian You have taken it wiselier than I meant you should.

Gonzalo Therefore, my lord, –

Antonio Fie, what a spendthrift is he of his tongue!

Alonso I prithee, spare.

Gonzalo Well, I have done: but yet, –

Sebastian He will be talking.

Antonio Which, of he or Adrian, for a good wager, first begins to crow?

Sebastian The old cock.

Antonio The cockerel.

Sebastian Done. The wager?

Antonio A laughter.

Sebastian A match!

Adrian Though this island seem to be desert –

Antonio Ha, ha, ha!

Sebastian So: you're paid!

Adrian Uninhabitable, and almost inaccessible –

Sebastian Yet –

Adrian Yet –

Gonzalo Peace *does* come to him, yes: you've spoken more truly than you intended.

Sebastian You've taken it more wisely than I intended.

Gonzalo [*resuming his weighty words of comfort*] Therefore, my lord –

Antonio My, how he does talk!

Alonso [*to* **Gonzalo**] Please: relax . . .

Gonzalo Well, I'll say no more. [*Pause*] However –

Sebastian He will keep talking!

[*There is a pause during which the entire party is silent*]

Antonio [*whispering to* **Sebastian**] For a good wager, who do you bet will start crowing first, he or Adrian?

Sebastian [*whispering back*] The old cock!

Antonio The cockerel!

Sebastian Done! [*They shake on it*] The wager?

Antonio The fun of it.

Sebastian It's a deal!

[*The silence continues*]

Adrian Though this island seems to be deserted –

Antonio [*laughing*] Ha, ha, ha!

Sebastian [*to* **Antonio**] So, you win!

Adrian [*continuing*] – uninhabitable and almost inaccessible –

Sebastian [*whispering in anticipation*] "Yet – "

Adrian – yet –

Antonio He could not miss 't.

Adrian It must needs be of subtle, tender and delicate temperance.

Antonio Temperance was a delicate wench.

Sebastian Ay, and a subtle; as he most learnedly delivered.

Adrian The air breathes upon us here most sweetly.

Sebastian As if it had lungs, and rotten ones.

Antonio Or as 'twere perfumed by a fen.

Gonzalo Here is everything advantageous to life.

Antonio True; save means to live.

Sebastian Of that there's none, or little.

Gonzalo How lush and lusty the grass looks! how green!

Antonio The ground, indeed, is tawny.

Sebastian With an eye of green in 't.

Antonio He misses not much.

Sebastian No; he doth but mistake the truth totally.

Gonzalo But the rarity of it is – which is indeed almost beyond credit –

Sebastian As many vouched rarities are.

Gonzalo That our garments, being, as they were, drenched in the sea, hold, notwithstanding, their freshness and glosses, being rather new-dyed than stained with salt water.

Antonio If but one of his pockets could speak, would it not say he lies?

Antonio [*whispering back*] He was bound to say that!

Adrian [*unaware his every word is being mocked*] – the weather must surely be mild, sweet, and pleasant.

Antonio [*nudging* **Sebastian**] I knew a girl who was like that.

Sebastian Yes, a real charmer, as he so learnedly said.

Adrian There's a breath of fresh air –

Sebastian [*aside to* **Antonio**] Straight from rotten lungs . . .

Antonio [*replying*] Or scented by a bog . . .

Gonzalo Everything one could wish for is here.

Antonio [*aside*] True: except the means to support life.

Sebastian [*aside*] There's little or nothing of that!

Gonzalo How lush and healthy the grass looks! How green!

Antonio [*aside*] The ground is parched, actually.

Sebastian [*aside*] With patches of green . . .

Antonio [*aside*] He doesn't miss much.

Sebastian [*aside*] No. Just the whole truth . . .

Gonzalo But the amazing thing is – and it's almost beyond belief –

Sebastian [*aside*] As so many amazing things are . . .

Gonzalo – that our clothes, though they were soaked in the sea, nevertheless still have their freshness and good appearance. They look freshly dyed rather than stained with salt water.

Antonio [*aside*] If just one of his pockets could speak, wouldn't it say he was lying?

Sebastian Ay, or very falsely pocket up his report.

Gonzalo Methinks our garments are now as fresh as when we put them on first in Afric, at the marriage of the King's fair daughter Claribel to the King of Tunis.

Sebastian 'Twas a sweet marriage, and we prosper well in our return.

Adrian Tunis was never graced before with such a paragon to their Queen.

Gonzalo Not since widow Dido's time.

Antonio Widow! a pox o' that! How came that widow in? Widow Dido!

Sebastian What if he had said 'widower Æneas' too? Good Lord, how you take it!

Adrian 'Widow Dido' said you? You make me study of that: she was of Carthage, not of Tunis.

Gonzalo This Tunis, sir, was Carthage.

Adrian Carthage?

Gonzalo I assure you, Carthage.

Antonio His word is more than the miraculous harp.

Sebastian He hath raised the wall, and houses too.

Antonio What impossible matter will he make easy next?

Sebastian I think he will carry this island home in his pocket, and give it his son for an apple.

Antonio And, sowing the kernels of it in the sea, bring forth more islands.

Sebastian [*aside*] Either that, or it would deceitfully pocket the evidence.

Gonzalo I do believe our garments are as fresh as when we first wore them in Africa, at the marriage of the king's gracious daughter Claribel to the king of Tunis.

Sebastian [*aside*] It was a lovely wedding, and we've had a splendid voyage back . . .

Adrian Tunis has never had such a beauty as its queen.

Gonzalo Not since the widow Dido's time.

Antonio [*aside*] Widow! Rubbish! Where did he get the "widow" from? "Widow" Dido indeed!

Sebastian [*aside*] What if he'd said "widower Aeneas" too? Good Lord, how it's possible to elaborate on things!

Adrian [*to* **Gonzalo**] Did you say "Widow Dido"? That makes me think: surely she was from Carthage, not Tunis?

Gonzalo Tunis used to be called Carthage.

Adrian Carthage?

Gonzalo Carthage, I assure you.

Antonio [*aside*] He's done more with words than Amphion did with his miraculous harp. When Amphion played, only the *walls* of Troy were created.

Sebastian [*aside*] He's invented the walls of Carthage and the houses too!

Antonio [*aside*] What will his next fantastic statement be?

Sebastian [*aside*] I think he'll carry this island home in his pocket and give it to his son as an apple.

Antonio [*aside*] And by sowing the seeds in the sea, make more islands!

Gonzalo Ay.

Antonio Why, in good time.

Gonzalo Sir, we were talking that our garments seem now as fresh as when we were at Tunis at the marriage of your daughter, who is now Queen.

Antonio And the rarest that e'er came there.

Sebastian Bate, I beseech you, widow Dido.

Antonio O, widow Dido! Ay, widow Dido.

Gonzalo Is not, sir, my doublet as fresh as the first day I wore it? I mean, in a sort.

Antonio That sort was well fished for.

Gonzalo When I wore it at your daughter's marriage?

Alonso You cram these words into mine ears against
The stomach of my sense. Would I had never
Married my daughter there! For, coming thence,
My son is lost, and, in my rate, she too,
Who is so far from Italy removed
I ne'er again shall see her. O thou mine heir
Of Naples and of Milan, what strange fish
Hath made his meal on thee?

Francisco Sir, he may live:
I saw him beat the surges under him,
And ride upon their backs; he trod the water,
Whose enmity he flung aside, and breasted
The surge most swoln that met him; his bold head
'Bove the contentious waves he kept, and oared
Himself with his good arms in lusty stroke
To th' shore, that o'er his wave-worn basis bowed,
As stooping to relieve him. I not doubt
He came alive to land.

Gonzalo [*still convinced that Tunis was once Carthage*] Oh, yes.

Antonio [*aside*] Quick thinking.

Gonzalo [*to* **Alonso**] Sir, we were saying that our clothes seem as fresh now as when we were at Tunis, at the marriage of your daughter, who is now the queen.

Antonio And the loveliest that ever went there.

Sebastian [*tongue in cheek*] With the exception, may I suggest, of widow Dido . . .

Antonio Oh, yes – widow Dido; yes, widow Dido!

Gonzalo Aren't my pants as fresh as the day I first wore them? [*He thinks a moment*] Relatively speaking, I mean –

Antonio That "relatively" was worth the deep thought.

Gonzalo When I wore them at your daughter's wedding?

Alonso You are forcing me to listen to things I'd rather forget! I wish I'd never let my daughter marry there! Because coming home, my son is drowned, and in my opinion she is lost too! She lives so far away from Italy I'll never see her again. Oh, my son and heir of Naples and Milan, what strange fish have you been food for?

Francisco Sir, he may be still alive. I saw him strike out strongly and ride the waves. He kept afloat, flinging aside the water and riding the heaving swell. He surfaced above the surging sea, keeping his bold head above the challenging waves and using his strong arms like oars to row his way to the shore, where cliffs sloped down toward him as if in rescue. I have no doubt he reached land alive.

Alonso No, no, he's gone.

Sebastian Sir, you may thank yourself for this great loss,
That would not bless our Europe with your daughter,
But rather loose her to an African;
Where she, at least, is banished from your eye,
Who hath cause to wet the grief on 't.

Alonso Prithee, peace.

Sebastian You were kneeled to, and importuned otherwise,
By all of us; and the fair soul herself
Weighed between loathness and obedience, at
Which end o' th' beam should bow. We have lost your son,
I fear, for ever: Milan and Naples have
More widows in them of this business' making
Than we bring men to comfort them:
The fault's your own.

Alonso So is the dear'st o' th' loss.

Gonzalo My lord Sebastian,
The truth you speak doth lack some gentleness,
And time to speak it in: you rub the sore,
When you should bring the plaster.

Sebastian Very well.

Antonio And most chirurgeonly.

Gonzalo It is foul weather in us all, good sir,
When you are cloudy.

Sebastian Foul weather?

Antonio Very foul.

Gonzalo Had I plantation of this isle, my lord, –

Antonio He'd sow 't with nettle-seed.

Sebastian Or docks, or mallows.

Alonso No, no. He's dead.

Sebastian Sir, you have yourself to thank for this great loss. You wouldn't give the continent of Europe the benefit of your daughter but chose instead to abandon her to an African. So you won't see her again, which is reason enough for weeping!

Alonso All right, all right.

Sebastian All of us begged and prayed you'd do otherwise. The poor girl was torn between reluctance to marry and a desire to obey, not knowing which to choose. I fear we have lost your son forever. In Milan and Naples more widows have been made by this business than there are survivors left to comfort them. The fault is all yours.

Alonso So is the greatest loss.

Gonzalo Lord Sebastian, your frankness is harsh and ill timed. You rub the sore when you should be applying a dressing.

Sebastian That's true.

Antonio Just like a surgeon!

Gonzalo A black mood in you means a nasty atmosphere for us all, dear sir.

Sebastian A nasty atmosphere?

Antonio Very nasty.

Gonzalo [*ignoring them*] If I settled here on this island, my lord –

Antonio [*aside*] He'd sow it with nettles.

Sebastian [*aside*] Or weeds or herbs.

Gonzalo And were the King on 't, what would I do?

Sebastian 'Scape being drunk for want of wine.

Gonzalo I' th' commonwealth I would by contraries
Execute all things; for no kind of traffic
Would I admit; no name of magistrate;
Letters should not be known; riches, poverty,
And use of service, none; contract, succession,
Bourn, bound of land, tilth, vineyard, none;
No use of metal, corn, or wine, or oil;
No occupation; all men idle, all;
And women too, but innocent and pure;
No sovereignty –

Sebastian Yet he would be king on 't!

Antonio The latter end of his commonwealth forgets the beginning.

Gonzalo All things in common Nature should produce
Without sweat or endeavour: treason, felony,
Sword, pike, knife, gun, or need of any engine,
Would I not have; but Nature should bring forth,
Of it own kind, all foison, all abundance,
To feed my innocent people.

Sebastian No marrying 'mong his subjects?

Antonio None, man; all idle; whores and knaves.

Gonzalo I would with such perfection govern, sir,
T' excel the Golden Age.

Sebastian Save his Majesty!

Antonio Long live Gonzalo!

Gonzalo And – do you mark me, sir?

Alonso Prithee, no more: thou dost talk nothing to me.

Gonzalo – and were its king, what would I do?

Sebastian [*aside*] Avoid being drunk through lack of wine!

Gonzalo I'd do everything by opposites in my perfect state. I'd allow no trade. There'd be no such thing as a magistrate. Learning would be unknown. No wealth, poverty, or slavery. No contracts, inheritances, boundaries, fences, cultivation of land, or vineyards. No use of metal, corn, wine, or oil. There'd be no occupations. All men would be idle: all of them. And all women too, but innocent and pure. There'd be no monarchy –

Sebastian [*aside*] Yet he said he'd be the king!

Antonio [*aside*] The final details of his system contradict those at the beginning!

Gonzalo Nature would produce all things without effort or labor, for the common good. I'd have no treason, law-breaking, swords, spears, knives, guns, or artillery. Nature would provide, by reproduction, all crops and harvests to feed my sinless people.

Sebastian [*aside*] Will there be no marrying among his subjects?

Antonio [*aside*] None, man; everyone idle: all prostitutes and villains.

Gonzalo So perfectly would I govern, sir, I'd surpass the Golden Age.

Sebastian [*saluting sarcastically*] God save His Majesty!

Antonio Long live Gonzalo! [*They laugh in derision*]

Gonzalo And – are you listening sir?

Alonso Please. No more. You are talking nonsense.

Gonzalo I do well believe your highness; and did it to minister occasion to these gentlemen, who are of such sensible and nimble lungs that they always use to laugh at nothing.

Antonio 'Twas you we laughed at.

Gonzalo Who in this kind of merry fooling am nothing to you; so you may continue, and laugh at nothing still.

Antonio What a blow was there given!

Sebastian An it had not fallen flat-long.

Gonzalo You are gentlemen of brave mettle; you would lift the moon out of her sphere, if she would continue in it five weeks without changing.

[*Enter* **Ariel**, *invisible, playing solemn music*]

Sebastian We would so, and then go a bat-fowling.

Antonio Nay, good my lord, be not angry.

Gonzalo No, I warrant you; I will not adventure my discretion so weakly. Will you laugh me asleep, for I am very heavy?

Antonio Go sleep, and hear us.

[*All sleep except* **Alonso, Sebastian** *and* **Antonio**]

Alonso What, all so soon asleep! I wish mine eyes
Would, with themselves, shut up my thoughts: I find
They are inclined to do so.

Sebastian Please you, sir,
Do not omit the heavy offer of it:
It seldom visits sorrow; when it doth,
It is a comforter.

Gonzalo Your Highness is quite right. I did so to give these gentlemen their chance; they have such sensitive and overactive lungs, they laugh at nothing.

Antonio It was you we were laughing at.

Gonzalo In this kind of silly behavior, I'm nothing compared with you. So carry on: keep laughing at nothing!

Antonio Wow! Such wit!

Sebastian Like a lead balloon.

Gonzalo How tough you gentlemen are! You'd lift the moon out of its orbit if it went five weeks without changing!

[**Ariel** *enters, invisible, playing solemn music*]

Sebastian We would that; and then do some moonlight poaching . . .

Antonio [*to* **Gonzalo**] My dear sir – don't be angry.

Gonzalo Indeed I won't. I wouldn't let a little thing like that disturb me. How about laughing me to sleep? I feel very tired.

Antonio Sleep by all means: are you listening? [*He laughs obligingly*]

[*Everyone falls asleep except* **Alonso, Sebastian,** *and* **Antonio**]

Alonso What, all asleep so soon? I wish I could shut out my thoughts by shutting my eyes. They're inclined to close.

Sebastian Well then, sir, don't resist the feeling. It doesn't often come to those in sorrow. When it does, it's a comfort.

Antonio We two, my lord,
Will guard your person while you take your rest,
And watch your safety.

Alonso Thank you. Wondrous heavy.

[**Alonso** *sleeps. Exit* **Ariel**]

Sebastian What a strange drowsiness possesses them!

Antonio It is the quality o' th' climate.

Sebastian Why
Doth it not then our eyelids sink? I find not
Myself disposed to sleep.

Antonio Nor I; my spirits are nimble.
They fell together all, as by consent;
They dropped, as by a thunder-stroke. What might,
Worthy Sebastian? O, what might? No more –
And yet methinks I see it in thy face,
What thou shouldst be; th' occasion speaks thee; and
My strong imagination sees a crown
Dropping upon thy head.

Sebastian What, art thou waking?

Antonio Do you not hear me speak?

Sebastian I do; and surely
It is a sleepy language, and thou speak'st
Out of thy sleep. What is it thou didst say?
This is a strange repose, to be asleep
With eyes wide open; standing, speaking, moving,
And yet so fast asleep.

Antonio Noble Sebastian,
Thou let'st thy fortune sleep – die, rather; wink'st
Whiles thou art waking.

Antonio We two, my lord, will guard you while you rest, and insure your safety.

Alonso Thank you. [*He yawns and stretches*] Amazingly sleepy . . .

[*He nods off quickly.* **Ariel** *leaves*]

Sebastian How remarkably drowsy they are!

Antonio It's the air here.

Sebastian So why doesn't it affect us? I'm not tired.

Antonio Nor am I. I feel wide awake. They all dropped off together, as if by mutual consent. They fell asleep as if a thunderbolt had struck them. [*He pauses, thinking*] What if, Sebastian, oh, what if – ? [*He stops short, not daring to express his thoughts*] I'd better say no more. [*His confidence returns*] And yet I think I can tell from your face what you should be . . . This is an ideal opportunity . . . I can see quite clearly a crown coming your way . . .

Sebastian Are you sure you're awake?

Antonio Can't you hear me speaking?

Sebastian I can. And surely it's just gabble, and you are talking in your sleep? What did you say? Yours is a strange sort of slumber, to be asleep with your eyes wide open: standing, speaking, moving about – and yet fast asleep.

Antonio Noble Sebastian, you are letting your *prospects* sleep – or should I say die! Your eyes are shut while you're awake!

Sebastian Thou dost snore distinctly;
There's meaning in thy snores.

Antonio I am more serious than my custom: you
Must be so too, if heed me; which to do
Trebles thee o'er.

Sebastian Well, I am standing water.

Antonio I'll teach you how to flow.

Sebastian Do so: to ebb
Hereditary sloth instructs me.

Antonio O,
If you but knew how you the purpose cherish
Whiles thus you mock it! How, in stripping it,
You more invest it! Ebbing men, indeed,
Most often do so near the bottom run
By their own fear or sloth.

Sebastian Prithee, say on:
The setting of thine eye and cheek proclaim
A matter from thee; and a birth, indeed,
Which throes thee much to yield.

Antonio Thus, sir:
Although this lord of weak remembrance, this,
Who shall be of as little memory
When he is earthed, hath here almost persuaded –
For he's a spirit of persuasion, only
Professes to persuade – the King his son's alive,
'Tis as impossible that he's undrowned
As he that sleeps here swims.

Sebastian I have no hope
That he's undrowned.

Antonio O, out of that 'no hope'
What great hope have you! No hope that way is

Sebastian Your snoring is articulate. There's meaning in the way you snore . . .

Antonio I'm more than usually serious. So must you be, if you take my advice. If you do, you'll be three times the man you are now.

Sebastian Well, I'm like still water – inclined neither one way nor the other.

Antonio I'll teach you how to flow . . .

Sebastian Please do. Being naturally lazy, I know how to ebb.

Antonio Oh, if you only knew the relevance of that flippant remark! How your self-analysis points to a solution! Fear and laziness always keep you ''ebbers'' down.

Sebastian Please go on: by the look in your eye and your flushed cheeks, there's something you've just got to say. You'll burst if you don't say it.

Antonio It's this, sir. [*Nodding toward* **Gonzalo**] Although this forgetful old lord here – who'll be forgotten himself when he's dead and buried – has almost persuaded the king that his son is still alive (it's his job to persuade, so he does so out of duty), it is just as impossible to suppose he's not drowned as it is to imagine that this fellow sleeping here is actually swimming.

Sebastian I have no hope of his survival.

Antonio Oh, what great hope stems from that ''no hope''! No

Another way so high a hope, that even
Ambition cannot pierce a wink beyond,
But doubt discovery there. Will you grant with me
That Ferdinand is drowned?

Sebastian He's gone.

Antonio Then tell me,
Who's the next heir of Naples?

Sebastian Claribel.

Antonio She that is Queen of Tunis; she that dwells
Ten leagues beyond man's life; she that from Naples
Can have no note, unless the sun were post –
The man i' th' moon's too slow – till new-born chins
Be rough and razorable; she that from whom
We all were sea-swallowed, though some cast again,
And that by destiny, to perform an act
Whereof what's past is prologue; what to come,
Is yours and my discharge.

Sebastian What stuff is this! How
say you?
'Tis true, my brother's daughter's Queen of Tunis;
So is she heir of Naples; 'twixt which regions
There is some space.

Antonio A space whose every cubit
Seems to cry out, 'How shall that Claribel
Measure us back to Naples? Keep in Tunis,
And let Sebastian wake.' Say this were death
That now hath seized them; why, they were no worse
Than now they are. There be that can rule Naples
As well as he that sleeps; lords that can prate
As amply and unnecessarily
As this Gonzalo; I myself could make
A chough of as deep chat. O, that you bore

hope in that direction is, from another point of view, so *high* a hope that even ambition can't look that far ahead, it's so mind-boggling. Do you concede that Ferdinand is drowned?

Sebastian He's dead.

Antonio Then tell me: who's next in line to the throne of Naples?

Sebastian Claribel.

Antonio She who is queen of Tunis, who lives more than a life time away; . . . who can't get news from Naples in less than fourteen years, unless the sun acts as postman – the man in the moon's too slow! The selfsame Claribel from whom we were going when we were shipwrecked. Some of us were cast ashore, destined to play a part in a drama. The prologue is past history. The plot is to be acted out by you and me.

Sebastian What nonsense is this? How do you mean? It's true my brother's daughter is queen of Tunis; she is heir to the throne of Naples, too; and there's a great distance between both places . . .

Antonio Every inch of which seems to cry "How can that Claribel make the journey back to Naples? So stay in Tunis, and let Sebastian wake up!" Suppose they had just been struck dead; they'd be no worse than they are now. There's someone who could rule Naples as well as the one who's sleeping here. There are plenty of lords who can prattle as long-windedly and unnecessarily as this Gonzalo. I could train a jackdaw to speak at his level. Oh, if only you thought

The mind that I do! What a sleep were this
For your advancement! Do you understand me?

Sebastian Methinks I do.

Antonio And how does your content
Tender your own good fortune?

Sebastian I remember
You did supplant your brother Prospero.

Antonio True:
And look how well my garments sit upon me;
Much feater than before: my brother's servants
Were then my fellows; now they are my men.

Sebastian But for your conscience.

Antonio Ay, sir; where lies that? if'twere a kibe,
'Twould put me to my slipper; but I feel not
This deity in my bosom: twenty consciences,
That stand 'twixt me and Milan, candied be they,
And melt, ere they molest! Here lies your brother,
No better than the earth he lies upon,
If he were that which now he's like, that's dead;
Whom I, with this obedient steel, three inches of it,
Can lay to bed for ever; whiles you, doing thus,
To the perpetual wink for aye might put
This ancient morsel, this Sir Prudence, who
Should not upbraid our course. For all the rest,
They'll take suggestion as a cat laps milk;
They'll tell the clock to any business that
We say befits the hour.

Sebastian Thy case, dear friend,
Shall be my precedent; as thou got'st Milan,
I'll come by Naples. Draw thy sword; one stroke
Shall free thee from the tribute which thou payest;
And I the King shall love thee.

as I do! What a sleep this would be [*pointing to* **Gonzalo, Alonso, Adrian,** *and* **Francisco**] in terms of your future prospects! Do you see what I mean?

Sebastian I think I do.

Antonio And how does this stroke of luck appeal to you?

Sebastian [*hedging his reply*] I remember you overthrew your brother, Prospero . . .

Antonio That's true. And look at the cut of my clothes now: far more stylish than before. My brother's servants were then my equals: now they are on my payroll.

Sebastian What about your conscience?

Antonio A good question, sir: where is it? If it were a corn, I'd be forced to wear a slipper. But I don't feel any sign of this divine faculty here in my heart. Twenty such consciences, all freezing cold, could stand between me and the throne of Milan before they'd trouble me. Here lies your brother. If he were dead, which is what he looks like now, he'd be no better than the earth he's lying on. [*He draws a dagger*] With three inches of this obedient steel I can put him to bed forever, while you – doing the same – could put this old gaffer, this "Sir Prim-and-Proper," who mustn't criticize our actions, to a perpetual forty winks. As for all the rest, they'll lap up our story like a cat drinks milk. They'll go along with anything we say.

Sebastian Your example will be my precedent, dear friend. Just as you got Milan, I'll acquire Naples. Draw your sword. One stroke will free you from the levy that you pay. I, the new king, will be your bosom friend.

Antonio Draw together;
And when I rear my hand, do you the like,
To fall it on Gonzalo.

Sebastian O, but one word.

[*They talk apart*]

[*Enter* **Ariel**, *with music and song*]

Ariel My master through his Art foresees the danger
That you, his friend, are in; and sends me forth –
For else his project dies – to keep them living.

[*He sings in* **Gonzalo***'s ear*]

While you here do snoring lie,
Open-ey'd conspiracy
His time doth take.
If of life you keep a care,
Shake off slumber, and beware:
Awake, awake!

Antonio Then let us both be sudden.

Gonzalo [*waking*] Now, good angels
Preserve the King!

[*The others wake*]

Alonso Why, how now? Ho; awake? Why are you drawn?
Wherefore this ghastly looking?

Gonzalo What's the matter?

Sebastian Whiles we stood here securing your repose,
Even now, we heard a hollow burst of bellowing
Like bulls, or rather lions; did't not wake you?
It struck mine ear most terribly.

Antonio Let us draw our swords simultaneously. When I raise my hand, you do the same, and bring it down on Gonzalo.

Sebastian Just one word more . . . [*He takes* **Antonio** *to one side*]

[**Ariel** *enters, still invisible. He goes to* **Gonzalo**]

Ariel Through his magic art, my master foresees the danger you, his friend, are in. He sends me to keep everyone alive; otherwise his plan will fail.

[*He sings in* **Gonzalo***'s ear*]

While you here do snoring lie,
Conspiracy with open eye
His chance does take.
If of life you have some care,
Shake off slumber, and beware.
Awake, awake!

Antonio [*returning, with sword raised*] So let's be quick!

Gonzalo [*suddenly snapping awake*] May the holy angels preserve the king!

[*The others wake up and look around in surprise*]

Alonso [*bewildered*] What's all this? Everyone awake? [*To* **Antonio**] Why have you drawn your sword? Why the ghastly looks?

Gonzalo What's the matter?

Sebastian [*dropping his sword and thinking quickly*] While we stood here guarding you as you slept, we heard a hollow burst of bellowing, like that of bulls, or rather, lions. Didn't it wake you up? It sounded fearful to me.

Alonso I heard nothing.

Antonio O, 'twas a din to fright a monster's ear,
To make an earthquake! Sure, it was the roar
Of a whole herd of lions.

Alonso Heard you this, Gonzalo?

Gonzalo Upon mine honour, sir, I heard a humming,
And that a strange one too, which did awake me:
I shaked you, sir, and cried; as mine eyes opened,
I saw their weapons drawn: there was a noise,
That's verily. 'Tis best we stand upon our guard,
Or that we quit this place. Let's draw our weapons.

Alonso Lead off this ground; and let's make further search
For my poor son.

Gonzalo Heavens keep him from these beasts!
For he is, sure, i' th' island.

Alonso Lead away.

Ariel Prospero my lord shall know what I have done:
So, King, go safely on to seek thy son.

[*Exeunt*]

Scene 2

Another part of the Island. Enter **Caliban**, *with a burthen of wood. A noise of thunder heard*

Caliban All the infections that the sun sucks up
From bogs, fens, flats, on Prosper fall, and make him

Alonso I heard nothing.

Antonio Oh, the din would have frightened a monster, caused an earthquake! It was surely the roar of a whole herd of lions!

Alonso Did you hear this, Gonzalo?

Gonzalo Upon my honor, sir, I heard a humming, and a rather strange one, too, which woke me up. I shook you, sir, and shouted out. As I opened my eyes, I saw their weapons were drawn. There was a noise, that's certain. We'd better be on our guard, or leave here. Let's draw our swords.

Alonso Lead the way, and let's continue the search for my poor son.

Gonzalo May the heavens keep him safe from these beasts – for he's surely on this island.

Alonso Lead the way.

Ariel My lord Prospero shall know what I have done. King, proceed in safety in search of your son.

[*They all leave*]

Scene 2

Another part of the island. **Caliban** *enters, carrying a load of wood. Thunder can be heard in the distance.*

Caliban May all the infections sucked up by the sun from bogs, fens, and swamps fall on Prospero, and give him a

By inch-meal a disease! His spirits hear me,
And yet I needs must curse. But they'll nor pinch,
Fright me with urchin-shows, pitch me i' th' mire,
Nor lead me, like a firebrand, in the dark
Out of my way, unless he bid 'em: but
For every trifle are they set upon me;
Sometime like apes, that mow and chatter at me,
And after bite me; then like hedgehogs, which
Lie tumbling in my barefoot way, and mount
Their pricks at my footfall; sometime am I
All wound with adders, who with cloven tongues
Do hiss me into madness.

[*Enter* **Trinculo**]

Lo, now, lo!
Here comes a spirit of his, and to torment me
For bringing wood in slowly. I'll fall flat;
Perchance he will not mind me.

Trinculo Here's neither bush nor shrub, to bear off any weather at all, and another storm brewing; I hear it sing i' th' wind. Yond same black cloud, yond huge one, looks like a foul bombard that would shed his liquor. If it should thunder as it did before, I know not where to hide my head: yond same cloud cannot choose but fall by pailfuls. What have we here? A man or a fish? Dead or alive? A fish: he smells like a fish; a very ancient and fish-like smell; a kind of, not of the newest Poor-John. A strange fish! Were I in England now, as once I was, and had but this painted, not a holiday fool there but would give a piece of silver: there would this monster make a man; any strange beast there makes a man; when they will not give a doit to relieve a lame beggar, they will lay out ten to see a dead Indian. Legged like a man! And his fins like arms! Warm o' my troth! I do now let loose my opinion, hold it no longer: this is no fish,

disease, little by little! His spirits can hear me, yet I can't stop cursing him. But they won't pinch me, or frighten me with ghosts, or throw me into the mud, or mislead me in the dark like a will-o'-the-wisp, unless he orders them to. They are set upon me for every little thing. Sometimes they make faces at me and chatter like apes, and then bite me. Sometimes they're like hedgehogs lying curled up in my way that, as I walk along in bare feet, raise their spines when I tread on them. Sometimes I'm twined around with adders, which hiss at me with forked tongues and drive me mad.

[**Trinculo***, a jester, enters*]

Look here, now, look! Here comes one of his spirits, to torment me for bringing the wood in so slowly. I'll lie flat. Perhaps he won't notice me.

Trinculo There are no bushes or shrubs here to keep off the weather at all, and there's another storm brewing. The wind's increasing. That black cloud yonder – that huge one – looks like a rotten cask that's about to burst open and shed its liquor. If it thunders like it did before, I don't know where I'll find cover. That cloud there is bound to rain bucketfuls. [*He sees* **Caliban**] What have we here? A man or a fish? Dead or alive? [*He sniffs*] A fish. He smells like a fish. A very ancient, fishy smell. A kind of [*he thinks hard*] not-the-most-recent salted hake. A queer fish! If I were in England now, as I was once, and I had this fish painted on a signboard, every idiot holidaymaker would pay me to see it. This monster would make a man's fortune there. Though they wouldn't give a farthing to help a lame beggar, they'll spend ten to see a dead Indian. [*He inspects* **Caliban** *more closely*] He has legs like a man! And his fins are like arms! [*He touches* **Caliban** *gingerly*] Warm, upon my word! I've changed my opinion; I don't hold it any longer; this isn't a fish. It's an islander, killed recently by a thunderbolt.

but an islander, that hath lately suffered by a thunderbolt. [*Thunder*] Alas, the storm is come again! My best way is to creep under his gaberdine; there is no other shelter hereabout; misery acquaints a man with strange bed-fellows. I will here shroud till the dregs of the storm be past.

[*Enter* **Stephano**, *singing, with a bottle in his hand*]

Stephano *I shall no more to sea, to sea,*
Here shall I die ashore –

This is a very scurvy tune to sing at a man's funeral; well, here's my comfort. [*He drinks*]

[*Sings*]
The master, the swabber, the boatswain, and I,
the gunner, and his mate,
Lov'd Mall, Meg, and Marian, and Margery,
But none of us cared for Kate;
For she had a tongue with a tang,
Would cry to a sailor, Go hang!
She loved not the savour of tar nor of pitch;
Yet a tailor might scratch her where'er she did itch.
Then to sea, boys, and let her go hang!

This is a scurvy tune too: but here's my comfort. [*He drinks*]

Caliban Do not torment me: O!

Stephano What's the matter? Have we devils here? Do you put tricks upon's with salvages and men of Ind, ha? I have

[*Thunder is heard, louder this time*] Alas, the storm's back again! I'd better creep under his cloak. There's no other shelter around here. Misfortune gives one strange bedfellows. I'll shelter here till the storm's over. [*He takes refuge alongside* **Caliban**]

[**Stephano** *enters. He carries a bottle in his hand and is the worse for drink. He is a butler by profession*]

Stephano [*singing*]
I shall no more to sea, to sea
Here shall I die, ashore –

That's a lousy song to sing at a man's funeral! [*He raises his bottle tipsily*] Well, here's my comfort! [*He takes a long drink*]

[*singing again*]
The captain, the deckhand, the bosun, and I,
The gunner, and his mate
Loved Moll, Meg, and Marion, and Margery,
But none of us cared for Kate,
'Cause she had a tongue with a tang.
She'd cry to a sailor "Go hang!"
She hated the smell both of tar and of pitch –
Though a tailor could scratch her wherever she itched!
So to sea, boys, and let her go hang!

This is a lousy tune, too. [*He raises the bottle to his lips again*] But here's my comfort!

Caliban [*to* **Trinculo**] Don't torment me! [*He groans*] Oh!

Stephano What's the matter? Do we have devils here? [*He inspects the bundle on the ground, from which two sets of legs protrude*] Is this some freak show, with savages and

not scaped drowning, to be afeard now of your four legs; for it hath been said: As proper a man as ever went on four legs cannot make him give ground; and it shall be said so again, while Stephano breathes at nostrils.

Caliban The spirit torments me: O!

Stephano This is some monster of the isle with four legs, who hath got, as I take it, an ague. Where the devil should he learn our language? I will give him some relief, if it be but for that. If I can recover him, and keep him tame, and get to Naples with him, he's a present for any emperor that ever trod on neat's-leather.

Caliban Do not torment me, prithee; I'll bring my wood home faster.

Stephano He's in his fit now, and does not talk after the wisest. He shall taste of my bottle; if he have never drunk wine afore, it will go near to remove his fit. If I can recover him, and keep him tame, I will not take too much for him; he shall pay for him that hath him and that soundly.

Caliban Thou dost me yet but little hurt; thou wilt anon, I know it by thy trembling: now Prosper works upon thee.

Stephano Come on your ways; open your mouth; here is that which will give language to you, cat. Open your mouth; this will shake your shaking, I can tell you, and that soundly: you cannot tell who's your friend: open your chaps again.

Trinculo I should know that voice: it should be – but he is drowned; and these are devils – O defend me!

men from India, eh? I haven't escaped drowning to be frightened now of your four legs. As the saying goes, ''As fine a man as ever walked with crutches wouldn't make this man turn and run'': it'll be said again as long as Stephano's alive!

Caliban [*as* **Trinculo** *wriggles about*] The spirit is tormenting me: oh!

Stephano This is some island monster with four legs who has a fever, I'd say. Where the devil did he learn our language? I'll give him some medicine, if that's all that's wrong with him. If I can make him better, and keep him tame, and get back to Naples with him, he'd be a present for any emperor who ever wore shoe leather.

Caliban [*to* **Trinculo**, *pleadingly*] Don't torment me, please! I'll bring the wood in faster!

Stephano He's in a fit now and isn't talking much sense. He can have a swig from my bottle. If he's never drunk wine before, it should help to cure his fit. If I can cure him and tame him, I won't ask too much for him: just every penny I can get! [*He staggers toward the crouching* **Caliban**]

Caliban [*alarmed by* **Trinculo**'*s trembling: from fear, as it happens, not possession by the devil as* **Caliban** *thinks*] You haven't hurt me yet, but I know you will from the way you are all of a quiver. Prospero is getting to work on you!

Stephano Come here: open your mouth. This'll get you talking – liquor makes a cat speak. Open your mouth: this'll stop your shaking, I can tell you: it really will. [**Caliban** *shrinks back*] You don't recognize a friend! Open your mouth again.

Trinculo I ought to know that voice! It's got to be – but he's drowned! These are devils! Oh, help!

Stephano Four legs and two voices, – a most delicate monster! His forward voice, now, is to speak well of his friend; his backward voice is to utter foul speeches and to detract. If all the wine in my bottle will recover him, I will help his ague. Come – Amen! I will pour some in thy other mouth.

Trinculo Stephano!

Stephano Doth thy other mouth call me? Mercy, mercy! This is a devil, and no monster: I will leave him; I have no lon· spoon.

Trinculo Stephano! If thou beest Stephano, touch me, and speak to me; For I am Trinculo – be not afeard – thy good friend Trinculo.

Stephano If thou beest Trinculo, come forth: I'll pull thee by the lesser legs: if any be Trinculo's legs, these are they. Thou art very Trinculo indeed! How cam'st thou to be the seige of this moon-calf? Can he vent Trinculos?

Trinculo I took him to be killed with a thunder-stroke. But art thou not drowned, Stephano? I hope, now, thou art not drowned. Is the storm over-blown? I hid me under the dead moon-calf's gaberdine for fear of the storm. And art thou living, Stephano? O Stephano, two Neapolitans 'scaped!

Stephano Prithee, do not turn me about; my stomach is not constant.

Caliban [*Aside*] These be fine things, an if they be not sprites. That's a brave god, and bears celestial liquor: I will kneel to him.

Stephano Four legs and two voices! What a subtle monster! His front voice is for speaking compliments, and his rear voice is for uttering abuse and criticism. If it takes all the wine in my bottle to save him, I'll cure his fever. Come. [*He pours wine down* **Caliban***'s throat*] That's enough! [*He moves to* **Trinculo***'s end*] I'll pour some into your other mouth.

Trinculo Stephano!

Stephano Is your other mouth calling me? [*He backs away in fear*] Mercy, mercy! This is a devil, not a monster. I'll leave him. Since I don't have a long spoon, I'll not eat with the devil.

Trinculo Stephano! If you're really Stephano, touch me and speak to me. I'm Trinculo. Don't be afraid – your good friend Trinculo!

Stephano If you are Trinculo, come out. [*He grips* **Trinculo** *firmly*] I'll pull you by the two small legs. If any belong to Trinculo, these do. [**Trinculo** *scrambles to his feet*] Trinculo, sure enough! How did you come to be a turd of this monstrosity? Can he excrete Trinculos?

Trinculo I thought he'd been killed by a thunderbolt. But weren't you drowned, Stephano? I hope you *aren't* drowned! Has the storm blown over? I hid myself under the dead monster's cloak for fear of the storm. So are you living, Stephano? Oh, Stephano – two Neapolitan survivors! [*He turns* **Stephano** *around to get a better view of him*]

Stephano [*stopping him*] Hey – don't spin me round. My stomach can't take it.

Caliban [*aside*] These are fine creatures if they aren't spirits. [*Nodding toward* **Stephano**] He's an excellent god, and he has heavenly liquor. I'll kneel to him.

Stephano How didst thou 'scape? How cam'st thou hither? Swear, by this bottle, how thou cam'st hither. I escaped upon a butt of sack, which the sailors heaved o'erboard, by this bottle! which I made of the bark of a tree with mine own hands, since I was cast ashore.

Caliban I'll swear, upon that bottle, to be thy true subject; for the liquor is not earthly.

Stephano Here; swear, then, how thou escap'dst.

Trinculo Swum ashore, man, like a duck: I can swim like a duck, I'll be sworn.

Stephano Here, kiss the book. Though thou canst swim like a duck, thou art made like a goose.

Trinculo O Stephano, hast any more of this?

Stephano The whole butt, man: my cellar is in a rock by th' sea-side, where my wine is hid. How now, moon-calf! How does thine ague?

Caliban Hast thou not dropped from heaven?

Stephano Out o' the moon, I do assure thee: I was the man i' th' moon when time was.

Caliban I have seen thee in her, and I do adore thee. My mistress showed me thee, and thy dog, and thy bush.

Stephano Come, swear to that; kiss the book: I will furnish it anon with new contents: swear.

Trinculo By this good light, this is a very shallow monster; I afeard of him? A very weak monster! The man i' th' moon! A most credulous monster! Well drawn, monster, in good sooth!

Stephano [*to* **Trinculo**] How did you escape? How did you get here? Swear on this bottle how you got here! I escaped on a cask of wine which the sailors threw overboard, by this bottle! [*He crosses himself with it*] I made it with my own hands from the bark of a tree after I was cast ashore.

Caliban [*groveling at* **Stephano**'*s feet*] I'll swear on that bottle to be your loyal subject. That liquor is divine!

Stephano [*handing the bottle to* **Trinculo** *as if it were a Bible*] Here. Swear how you escaped.

Trinculo I swam ashore, man, like a duck. I can swim like a duck, I assure you!

Stephano [*offering* **Trinculo** *a drink*] Here. Take a swig! Though you can swim like a duck, you're a bit of a goose.

Trinculo [*wiping his mouth*] Oh, Stephano: have you any more of this?

Stephano The whole cask, man. My cellar is in a cave by the seaside, where my wine is hid. [*Noticing the groveling* **Caliban**] Well now, monster! How's your fever?

Caliban [*adoringly*] Have you come from heaven?

Stephano From the moon, as a matter of fact. I was the man in the moon once upon a time . . .

Caliban I've seen you in her, and I adore you. My mistress showed you to me, and your dog, and your bush.

Stephano [*pressing more drink on* **Caliban**] Come on: swear to that. Take a swig. [**Caliban** *drinks thirstily*] I'll fill it up again later. Swear!

Trinculo By god, this is a very foolish monster. Me afraid of him? A very stupid monster! [*He scoffs*] The man in the moon! A very naïve monster! [*After a very long drink* **Caliban** *lowers the bottle*] Well drunk, monster, by god!

Caliban I'll show thee every fertile inch o' th' island; and I will kiss thy foot. I prithee, be my god.

Trinculo By this light, a most perfidious and drunken monster! When's god's asleep, he'll rob his bottle.

Caliban I'll kiss thy foot; I'll swear myself thy subject.

Stephano Come on, then; down, and swear.

Trinculo I shall laugh myself to death at this puppy-headed monster. A most scurvy monster! I could find in my heart to beat him –

Stephano Come, kiss.

Trinculo But that the poor monster's in drink. An abominable monster!

Caliban I'll show thee the best springs; I'll pluck thee berries;
I'll fish for thee, and get thee wood enough.
A plague upon the tyrant that I serve!
I'll bear him no more sticks, but follow thee,
Thou wondrous man.

Trinculo A most ridiculous monster, to make a wonder of a poor drunkard!

Caliban I prithee, let me bring thee where crabs grow;
And I with my long nails will dig thee pig-nuts;
Show thee a jay's nest, and instruct thee how
To snare the nimble marmoset; I'll bring thee
To clustering filberts, and sometimes I'll get thee
Young scamels from the rock. Wilt thou go with me?

Stephano I prithee now, lead the way, without any more talking. Trinculo, the King and all our company else being drowned, we will inherit here. Here; bear my bottle. Fellow Trinculo, we'll fill him by and by again.

Caliban [*to* **Stephano**] I'll show you every fertile inch of the island, and I'll kiss your feet. Please, be my god! [*He reaches out for the bottle as* **Stephano** *nods off*]

Trinculo By heavens, a really wicked and drunken monster. When his god's asleep, he'd steal his bottle! [*He gives* **Stephano** *a shake*]

Caliban I'll kiss your feet. I'll swear to be your subject.

Stephano Come on, then: down and swear! [**Caliban** *drops to his knees*]

Trinculo I'll laugh myself to death at this dim-witted monster. What a rascally monster! I could thump him –

Stephano Come on – kiss!

Trinculo – but the poor monster is drunk. A loathsome monster!

Caliban [*groveling*] I'll show you the freshest springs. I'll collect berries for you. I'll fish for you and get you all the wood you need. Damn the tyrant that I serve! I'll carry no more logs for him, but serve you, you marvelous man!

Trinculo A truly ridiculous monster, to worship a drunkard!

Caliban Please, let me take you to where the apples grow. With my long nails I'll dig up groundnuts. I'll show you a jay's nest and teach you how to trap a nimble little monkey. I'll take you to clusters of nuts, and sometimes I'll get you young seagulls from the rocks. Will you go with me?

Stephano Right, then; lead the way without another word. Trinculo, the king and the rest of our company being drowned, we'll take over this place. Here: [*he hands his bottle to* **Trinculo**] carry my bottle. Trinculo, my man, we'll refill it shortly.

Caliban [*sings drunkenly*] Farewell, master; farewell, farewell!

Trinculo A howling monster; a drunken monster!

Caliban [*singing*]
No more dams I'll make for fish;
Nor fetch in firing
At requiring;
Nor scrape trenchering, nor wash dish:
'Ban, 'Ban, Cacaliban
Has a new master – get a new man.

Freedom, high-day! high-day, freedom! freedom, high-day, freedom!.

Stephano O brave monster! Lead the way.

[*Exeunt*]

Caliban [*singing drunkenly*] Farewell, master, farewell!

Trinculo [*his hands over his ears*] A howling monster! A drunken monster!

Caliban [*singing*]

I'll make no dams for catching fish;
Fetch in no kindling
At his bidding;
Nor scrape his plates, nor wash a dish;
'Ban, 'Ban, Cacaliban
Has a new master: get a new man!

Freedom, liberty! Liberty, freedom! Freedom, liberty, freedom!

Stephano You brave monster! Lead the way!

[*They go*]

Act three

Scene 1

Before Prospero's Cell. Enter **Ferdinand**, *bearing a log*

Ferdinand There be some sports are painful, and their labour
Delight in them sets off: some kinds of baseness
Are nobly undergone; and most poor matters
Point to rich ends. This my mean task
Would be as heavy to me as odious, but
The mistress which I serve quickens what's dead,
And makes my labours pleasures. O, she is
Ten times more gentle than her father's crabbed,
And he's composed of harshness. I must remove
Some thousands of these logs, and pile them up,
Upon a sore injunction: my sweet mistress
Weeps when she sees me work, and says, such baseness
Had never like executor. I forget:
But these sweet thoughts do even refresh my labours,
Most busilest when I do it.

[*Enter* **Miranda**; *and* **Prospero**, *at a distance, unseen*]

Miranda Alas now, pray you,
Work not so hard: I would the lightning had
Burnt up those logs that you are enjoined to pile!
Pray, set it down, and rest you: when this burns,
'Twill weep for having wearied you. My father
Is hard at study; pray, now, rest yourself:
He's safe for these three hours.

Ferdinand O most dear mistress,
The sun will set before I shall discharge
What I must strive to do.

Act three

Scene 1

In front of Prospero's cave. **Ferdinand** *enters, carrying a log.*

Ferdinand Some sports are strenuous, but the effort is offset by the pleasure they give. Some humble labor has dignity. Most mundane occupations have worthwhile purposes. My menial task would be as tedious to me as it is unpleasant, if it were not for the mistress I work for. She enlivens what would otherwise be boring, and makes my toil a pleasure. Oh, she's ten times gentler than her father is: he is harshness through and through. I have to move thousands of these logs and pile them up under threat of punishment. My sweet mistress weeps when she sees me work and says no such laboring was ever done by one so noble. I'm day-dreaming: these pleasant thoughts give me renewed energy. I work at my hardest when my mind's occupied elsewhere.

[**Miranda** *enters, followed at a distance by* **Prospero**, *whom she cannot see.* **Ferdinand** *is struggling with a large log*]

Miranda Alas, don't work so hard, I beg you! I wish the lightning had set fire to these logs you've been ordered to pile up! Please, put that one down and take a rest. When this burns, it will cry for having tired you out. My father is busy studying. Please, do rest yourself. He's safe for the next three hours.

Ferdinand O dear mistress, it will be sunset before I've completed my task.

Miranda If you'll sit down,
I'll bear your logs the while: pray give me that;
I'll carry it to the pile.

Ferdinand No, precious creature;
I had rather crack my sinews, break my back,
Than you should such dishonour undergo,
While I sit lazy by.

Miranda It would become me
As well as it does you: and I should do it
With much more ease; for my good will is to it,
And yours it is against.

Prospero Poor worm, thou art infected!
This visitation shows it.

Miranda You look wearily.

Ferdinand No, noble mistress: 'tis fresh morning with me
When you are by at night. I do beseech you –
Chiefly that I might set it in my prayers –
What is your name?

Miranda Miranda. O my father,
I have broke your hest to say so!

Ferdinand Admired Miranda!
Indeed the top of admiration! worth
What's dearest to the world! Full many a lady
I have eyed with best regard, and many a time
Th' harmony of their tongues hath into bondage
Brought my too diligent ear: for several virtues
Have I liked several women; never any
With so full soul, but some defect in her
Did quarrel with the noblest grace she owed,
And put it to the foil: but you, O you,
So perfect and so peerless, are created
Of every creature's best!

Miranda If you'll sit down, I'll carry your logs meanwhile. Please, give that to me. I'll carry it to the pile. [*She tries to relieve* **Ferdinand** *of his burden*]

Ferdinand [*resisting*] No, precious one. I'd rather strain my muscles, break my back, than see you so humiliated while I sit idly by.

Miranda It would become me as well as it does you, and I'd do it with much more ease. My heart would be in it, whereas yours isn't.

Prospero [*overhearing*] Poor creature; you've caught it badly. This visit proves it.

Miranda You look exhausted.

Ferdinand No, noble mistress. It's like early morning to me when you're nearby at night. May I ask – chiefly so that I can include it in my prayers – what is your name?

Miranda Miranda. [*She claps her hand to her mouth*] Oh, father! I've disobeyed your orders in saying so!

Ferdinand Admired Miranda! Supremely admirable! Most precious in all the world! I've admired many women and often their sweet words have made me fall in love. For various qualities I've liked various women; never has one of them been so perfect that there wasn't some defect in her that stood out in contrast with her virtues. But you – oh, you! – so perfect, so without equal – you are composed of the finest features of each of them!

Miranda I do not know
One of my sex; no woman's face remember,
Save, from my glass, mine own; nor have I seen
More that I may call men than you, good friend,
And my dear father: how features are abroad,
I am skilless of; but, by my modesty,
The jewel in my dower, I would not wish
Any companion in the world but you;
Nor can imagination form a shape,
Besides yourself, to like of. But I prattle
Something too wildly, and my father's precepts
I therein do forget.

Ferdinand I am, in my condition,
A prince, Miranda; I do think, a King –
I would not so – and would no more endure
This wooden slavery than to suffer
The flesh-fly blow my mouth. Hear my soul speak:
The very instant that I saw you, did
My heart fly to your service; there resides,
To make me slave to it; and for your sake
Am I this patient log-man.

Miranda Do you love me?

Ferdinand O heaven, O earth, bear witness to this sound,
And crown what I profess with kind event,
If I speak true! If hollowly, invert
What best is boded me to mischief! I,
Beyond all limit of what else i' th' world,
Do love, prize, honour you.

Miranda I am a fool
To weep at what I am glad of.

Prospero Fair encounter
Of two most rare affections! Heavens rain grace
On that which breeds between 'em!

Miranda I do not know another woman. I can't recall a woman's face, except my own that I see in my mirror. Nor have I seen another real man besides you, good friend, and my dear father. What people look like in the world in general, I do not know. But upon my modesty – my most precious possession – I wouldn't wish any other companion in the world but you. Nor can my imagination conceive of anyone to like more than I do you. But I'm prattling away rather too wildly and therein forgetting my father's instructions.

Ferdinand In rank, Miranda, I'm a prince. Probably a king, though I wish I were not. I would no more tolerate this wood-carrying slavery than I'd let a blowfly foul my mouth. Hear my soul speak: I loved you at first sight. I am your slave. For your sake, I'm this patient log carrier.

Miranda Do you love me?

Ferdinand Heaven and earth be witness to my words. If I'm speaking the truth, may my vows be crowned with success. If I'm lying, may any happiness that's due to me become misfortune! I love, value, honor you more than anything else in the world!

Miranda [*wiping a tear*] I'm a fool to weep at what's so good to hear.

Prospero [*aside*] A joyous meeting of two kindred souls! May good fortune be theirs in their union!

Ferdinand Wherefore weep you?

Miranda At mine unworthiness, that dare not offer
What I desire to give; and much less take
What I shall die to want. But this is trifling;
And all the more it seeks to hide itself,
The bigger bulk it shows. Hence, bashful cunning!
And prompt me plain and holy innocence!
I am your wife if you will marry me;
If not, I'll die your maid: to be your fellow
You may deny me; but I'll be your servant,
Whether you will or no.

Ferdinand My mistress, dearest;
And I thus humble ever.

Miranda My husband, then?

Ferdinand Ay, with a heart as willing
As bondage e'er of freedom: here's my hand.

Miranda And mine, with my heart in 't: and now farewell
Till half an hour hence.

Ferdinand A thousand thousand!

[*Exeunt* **Ferdinand** *and* **Miranda**, *severally*]

Prospero So glad of this as they I cannot be,
Who are surprised with all; but my rejoicing
At nothing can be more. I'll to my book;
For yet, ere supper-time, must I perform
Much business appertaining.

[*Exit*]

Ferdinand Why are you crying?

Miranda At my unworthiness. [*She blushes and answers the question indirectly out of modesty*] I daren't offer you what I'd like to give. Far less can I take what I can't live without. [*She pauses, then decides that conundrums don't suit the occasion*] This is silly. The more I try to hide things, the more obvious they seem. No more bashful riddles! The truth, pure and simple! I'll be your wife, if you will marry me. If not, I'll die unmarried. You can reject me as your partner. But I'll be your servant whether you want me or not.

Ferdinand My *wife*, dearest! [*He kneels*] Yours, evermore!

Miranda My husband, then?

Ferdinand Yes, as willingly as a slave seeks freedom. Here is my hand.

Miranda And mine, and with it my heart. And now, farewell till half an hour from now.

Ferdinand A thousand, thousand farewells!

[*They go their separate ways*]

Prospero I can't be as overjoyed at this as they: it took them by surprise. But nothing could give me greater pleasure. I must return to my magic book. Before suppertime, I've a lot of things to do.

[*He leaves*]

Scene 2

Another part of the Island. Enter **Caliban, Stephano** *and* **Trinculo**

Stephano Tell not me – when the butt is out, we will drink water; not a drop before: therefore bear up, and board 'em. Servant-monster, drink to me.

Trinculo Servant-monster! The folly of this island! They say there's but five upon this isle: we are three of them; if th' other two be brained like us, the state totters.

Stephano Drink, servant-monster, when I bid thee: thy eyes are almost set in thy head.

Trinculo Where should they be set else? He were a brave monster indeed, if they were set in his tail.

Stephano My man-monster hath drowned his tongue in sack: for my part, the sea cannot drown me; I swam, ere I could recover the shore, five-and-thirty leagues off and on. By this light, thou shalt be my lieutenant, monster, or my standard.

Trinculo Your lieutenant, if you list; he's no standard.

Stephano We'll not run, Monsieur Monster.

Trinculo Nor go neither; but you'll lie, like dogs; and yet say nothing neither.

Stephano Moon-calf, speak once in thy life, if thou beest a good moon-calf.

Caliban How does thy honour? Let me lick thy shoe: I'll not serve him, he is not valiant.

Scene 2

Another part of the island. **Caliban, Stephano,** *and* **Trinculo** *enter.*

Stephano All right! When we've finished the cask, we'll drink water, but not a drop before. So cheers, and bottoms up! [*He takes a long drink*] Servant-monster, drink to me!

Trinculo Servant-monster! The island freak! They say there's only five on this isle. We're three of them. If the other two are as crazy as we are, the country's in a terrible state.

Stephano Drink, servant-monster, when I tell you to. Your eyes are almost fixed in your head.

Trinculo Where else could they be fixed? He'd be a remarkable monster indeed if they were fixed in his tail! [**Caliban** *is too drunk to reply*]

Stephano My man-monster has drowned his tongue in wine. As for me, the sea can't drown me! Before I reached shore, I swam thirty-five leagues, off and on. [*To* **Caliban**] By heaven, you can be my lieutenant – or my standard-bearer.

Trinculo Your lieutenant, if you please. He can't stand upright!

Stephano We'll stand our ground, Mr. Monster! [*He helps to prop* **Caliban** *up, but they fall in a heap*]

Trinculo You can't walk, that's for sure – you'll have to lie there like dogs and not say a word.

Stephano Monster: speak for once in your life, if you're a good monster.

Caliban How is my lord? Let me lick your shoe. [*Nodding in* **Trinculo***'s direction*] I won't serve him. He's a coward.

Trinculo Thou liest, most ignorant monster: I am in case to jostle a constable. Why, thou deboshed fish, thou, was there ever man a coward that hath drunk so much sack as I to-day? Wilt thou tell a monstrous lie, being but half a fish and half a monster?

Caliban Lo, how he mocks me! Wilt thou let him, my lord?

Trinculo 'Lord,' quoth he? That a monster should be such a natural!

Caliban Lo, lo, again! Bite him to death, I prithee.

Stephano Trinculo, keep a good tongue in your head: if you prove a mutineer – the next tree! The poor monster's my subject, and he shall not suffer indignity.

Caliban I thank my noble lord. Wilt thou be pleased to hearken once again to the suit I made to thee?

Stephano Marry, will I: kneel and repeat it; I will stand, and so shall Trinculo.

[*Enter* **Ariel**, *invisible*]

Caliban As I told thee before, I am subject to a tyrant, a sorcerer, that by his cunning hath cheated me of the island.

Ariel Thou liest.

Caliban 'Thou liest,' thou jesting monkey, thou!
I would my valiant master would destroy thee!
I do not lie.

Stephano Trinculo, if you trouble him any more in 's tale, by this hand, I will supplant some of your teeth.

Trinculo Why, I said nothing.

Trinculo You're lying, you ignorant monster! I've enough courage to shove a policeman. Why, you randy fish you, was any man ever a coward who'd drunk as much wine as I have today? How dare you tell a monstrous lie when you're only half fish and half monster!

Caliban [*to* **Stephano**] Listen how he mocks me! Will you let him, my lord?

Trinculo "Lord," he said! Fancy a monster being such an idiot!

Caliban Listen, listen! He's at it again. Bite him to death, I beg of you!

Stephano Trinculo, keep a respectful tongue in your head. If you turn mutinous it's the next tree for you. The poor monster is one of my subjects, and he mustn't be humiliated.

Caliban I thank my noble lord. Would it be your pleasure to listen again to my humble petition?

Stephano Indeed I will. Kneel, and repeat it. I'll stand, and so will Trinculo.

[**Ariel** *enters, invisible*]

Caliban As I told you before, I'm subject to a tyrant, a magician, who has cheated me of this island by his cleverness.

Ariel Liar!

Caliban [*thinking* **Trinculo** *has spoken*] *You're* lying, you cheeky monkey, you! I wish my valiant master would destroy you. I don't lie!

Stephano Trinculo, if you interrupt his story again, I'll knock out some of your teeth, I will.

Trinculo Why? I didn't say anything!

Stephano Mum, then, and no more. Proceed.

Caliban I say, by sorcery he got this isle;
From me he got it. If thy greatness will
Revenge it on him – for I know thou dar'st,
But this thing dare not –

Stephano That's most certain.

Caliban Thou shalt be lord of it, and I'll serve thee.

Stephano How now shall this be compassed? Canst thou bring me to the party?

Caliban Yea, yea, my lord: I'll yield him thee asleep,
Where thou mayst knock a nail into his head.

Ariel Thou liest; thou canst not.

Caliban What a pied ninny's this! Thou scurvy patch!
I do beseech thy greatness, give him blows,
And take his bottle from him: when that's gone,
He shall drink nought but brine; for I'll not show him
Where the quick freshes are.

Stephano Trinculo, run into no further danger: interrupt the monster one word further, and, by this hand, I'll turn my mercy out o' doors, and make a stock-fish of thee.

Trinculo Why, what did I? I did nothing. I'll go farther off.

Stephano Didst thou not say he lied?

Ariel Thou liest.

Stephano Do I so? Take thou that. [*Beats him*] As you like this, give me the lie another time.

Trinculo I did not give the lie. Out o' your wits, and hearing too? A pox o' your bottle! This can sack and drinking do. A

Stephano Quiet, then. Let's have no more. [*To* **Caliban**] Continue . . .

Caliban I was saying that by his magic he got this island. He took it from me. If Your Greatness will take revenge on him – because I know you dare, whereas this thing [*he means* **Trinculo**] is too scared –

Stephano That's for sure!

Caliban – you can be lord of it, and I'll serve you.

Stephano How can we do it, now? Can you take me to the person in question?

Caliban Yes, yes, my lord: I'll betray him to you while he's asleep, so then you can dash his brains out.

Ariel You're lying. You can't.

Caliban [*again thinking that* **Trinculo** *has spoken*] What a jibbering idiot he is! You insolent clown! [*To* **Stephano**] I beg Your Greatness: beat him, and take away his bottle. When that's gone, he'll have to drink salt water, for I won't show him where the fast-flowing streams are.

Stephano Trinculo, watch it! Interrupt the monster once more and, by all that's holy, I'll have no mercy on you: I'll beat you to a pulp.

Trinculo Why, what did I do? I didn't do anything! I'll go further away.

Stephano Didn't you say he lied?

Ariel *You* lie . . .

Stephano Oh, do I? Take that! [*He beats* **Trinculo** *over the head*] If you liked that, call me a liar again!

Trinculo I didn't call you a liar. Have you lost your wits and your hearing too? Damn your bottle! This is what wine and

murrain on your monster, and the devil take your fingers!

Caliban Ha, ha, ha!

Stephano No, forward with your tale. Prithee, stand further off.

Caliban Beat him enough: after a little time,
I'll beat him too.

Stephano Stand farther. Come, proceed.

Caliban Why, as I told thee, 'tis a custom with him
I' th' afternoon to sleep: there thou mayst brain him,
Having first seized his books; or with a log
Batter his skull, or paunch him with a stake,
Or cut his wezand with thy knife. Remember
First to possess his books; for without them
He's but a sot, as I am, nor hath not
One spirit to command: they all do hate him
As rootedly as I. Burn but his books.
He has brave utensils – for so he calls them –
Which, when he has a house, he'll deck withal.
And that most deeply to consider is
The beauty of his daughter; he himself
Calls her a nonpareil: I never saw a woman,
But only Sycorax my dam and she;
But she as far surpasseth Sycorax
As great'st does least.

Stephano Is it so brave a lass?

Caliban Ay, lord; she will become thy bed, I warrant,
And bring thee forth brave brood.

Stephano Monster, I will kill this man: his daughter and I will be king and queen – save our graces! – and Trinculo and thyself shall be viceroys. Dost thou like the plot, Trinculo?

drinking can do. Blast your monster, and the devil take your fingers!

Caliban Ha, ha, ha!

Stephano [*to* **Caliban**] Now carry on with your story. [*To* **Trinculo**] Please, stand further away.

Caliban Beat him soundly. After a bit, I'll beat him too!

Stephano [*to* **Trinculo**, *pointing*] Further still. [*To* **Caliban**] Right. Carry on.

Caliban Well, as I told you, it's his custom to sleep in the afternoon. There you could smash his brains in, after you've seized his books. Or you could batter his skull with a log, or run him through the stomach with a stake, or cut his throat with your knife. But remember to get his books first. Without them he's just a nobody as I am, without a single spirit at his command: they all hate him as thoroughly as I do. Be sure to burn his books. He has fine "utensils," as he calls them, which are for equipping his house when he gets one. But what's worth thinking about most is the beauty of his daughter. He himself says she has no equal. I've only seen two women – my mother Sycorax and her – but his daughter far surpasses Sycorax, as the greatest outshines the least.

Stephano Is she so beautiful?

Caliban Yes, lord, and she'll be good in bed, I guarantee you, and you'll have a fine lot of children.

Stephano Monster, I will kill this man. His daughter and I will be king and queen – God save Our Graces! – and Trinculo and you will be viceroys. Do you like the plot, Trinculo?

Trinculo Excellent.

Stephano Give me thy hand: I am sorry I beat thee; but, while thou liv'st, keep a good tongue in thy head.

Caliban Within this half hour will he be asleep:
Wilt thou destroy him then?

Stephano Ay, on mine honour.

Ariel This will I tell my master.

Caliban Thou mak'st me merry; I am full of pleasure:
Let us be jocund: will you troll the catch
You taught me but the while-ere?

Stephano At thy request, monster, I will do reason, any reason. Come on, Trinculo, let us sing.

[*Sings*]
Flout 'em and scout 'em,
And scout 'em and flout 'em;
Thought is free.

Caliban That's not the tune.

[**Ariel** *plays the tune on a tabor and pipe*]

Stephano What is this same?

Trinculo This is the tune of our catch, played by the picture of Nobody.

Stephano If thou beest a man, show thyself in thy likeness: if thou beest a devil, take 't as thou list.

Trinculo O, forgive me my sins!

Stephano He that dies pays all debts: I defy thee. Mercy upon us!

Trinculo Excellent!

Stephano Give me your hand. I'm sorry I beat you, but be a good fellow and keep your tongue under control.

Caliban Within half an hour he'll be asleep. Will you kill him then?

Stephano Yes, upon my honor.

Ariel I'll tell my master this.

Caliban You make me very happy. I'm really pleased. Let's be cheerful. Shall we try out the song you taught me a while back?

Stephano For you, monster, I will do anything, anything. Come on, Trinculo. Let's sing.

[*singing*]
Mock 'em and sock 'em
And sock 'em and mock 'em;
Thought is free –

Caliban That's not the tune!

[**Ariel** *plays the tune on a drum and a pipe. The revelers stop and listen in surprise*]

Stephano What's all this?

Trinculo [*trembling*] This is the tune of our song, played by the invisible man.

Stephano [*shouting defiantly*] If you're a man, show yourself as you are. If you're a devil, choose what shape you like!

Trinculo [*down on his knees*] Oh, forgive me my sins!

Stephano The man who dies pays all his debts: I defy you. [*He crosses himself just the same*] Mercy on us!

Caliban Art thou afeard?

Stephano No, monster, not I.

Caliban Be not afeard; the isle is full of noises,
Sounds and sweet airs, that give delight, and hurt not.
Sometimes a thousand twangling instruments
Will hum about mine ears; and sometime voices,
That, if I then had wak'd after long sleep,
Will make me sleep again: and then, in dreaming,
The clouds methought would open, and show riches
Ready to drop upon me; that, when I wak'd,
I cried to dream again.

Stephano This will prove a brave kingdom to me, where I shall have my music for nothing.

Caliban When Prospero is destroyed.

Stephano That shall be by and by: I remember the story.

Caliban The sound is going away; let's follow it, and after do our work.

Stephano Lead, monster; we'll follow. I would I could see this taborer; he lays it on. Wilt come?

Trinculo I'll follow, Stephano.

[*Exeunt*]

Caliban Are you afraid?

Stephano [*shivering, but not admitting it*] No, monster, not I.

Caliban Don't be afraid. The island is full of noises, sounds, and sweet tunes that give delight and don't hurt. Sometimes the sound of a thousand twangling instruments will hum in my ears, and sometimes voices, which, if I awaken after a long sleep, will put me to sleep again. Then, in my dreams, the clouds seem to open and reveal riches ready to fall on me, so that when I wake, I cry to dream again.

Stephano This will be a splendid kingdom for me. I'll have free music!

Caliban When Prospero is destroyed . . .

Stephano That will be soon. I haven't forgotten the story.

Caliban The sound is going away. Let's follow it, and do our work afterwards.

Stephano Lead on, monster. We'll follow you. I wish I could see this drummer. He has a good beat. [*To* **Trinculo**] Are you coming?

Trinculo After you, Stephano!

[*They leave*]

Scene 3

Another part of the Island. Enter **Alonso, Sebastian, Antonio, Gonzalo, Adrian, Francisco,** *and others*

Gonzalo By'r lakin, I can go no further, sir;
My old bones ache: here's a maze trod, indeed,
Through forth-rights and meanders! By your patience,
I needs must rest me.

Alonso Old lord, I cannot blame thee,
Who am myself attached with weariness,
To th' dulling of my spirits: sit down, and rest.
Even here I will put off my hope, and keep it
No longer for my flatterer: he is drowned
Whom thus we stray to find; and the sea mocks
Our frustrate search on land. Well, let him go.

Antonio [*Aside to* **Sebastian**] I am right glad that he's so out of hope.
Do not, for one repulse, forego the purpose
That you resolved t' effect.

Sebastian [*Aside to* **Antonio**] The next advantage
Will we take throughly.

Antonio [*Aside to* **Sebastian**] Let it be to-night;
For, now they are oppressed with travel, they
Will not, nor cannot, use such vigilance
As when they are fresh.

Sebastian [*Aside to* **Antonio**] I say, to-night: no more.

[*Solemn and strange music;* **Prospero** *enters, invisible. Enter several strange Shapes, bringing in a banquet; they dance about it with gentle actions of salutations; inviting the King, etc. to eat, they depart*]

Scene 3

Another part of the island. **Alonso, Sebastian, Antonio, Gonzalo, Adrian, Francisco,** *and others enter.*

Gonzalo To be sure, I can go no further, sir. My old bones ache. What a maze we've walked, along straight and meandering paths! If you'll excuse me, I just have to rest.

Alonso Old lord, I can't blame you. Weariness has seized me; I'm exhausted. Sit down and rest. Here I abandon all hope; it sustains me no longer. My son is drowned, and the sea mocks our vain search on land. Well, he is gone.

Antonio [*to* **Sebastian**] I'm very glad he's given up hope. Just because of that one setback, don't change your plans.

Sebastian [*to* **Antonio**] We'll take the next opportunity.

Antonio [*to* **Sebastian**] Make that tonight. Being so tired with traveling, they neither will nor can be so watchful as when they're fresh.

Sebastian [*to* **Antonio**] Tonight, then. Say no more.

[*Solemn and unusual music is heard.* **Prospero** *enters, invisible. Several* **Spirits** *bring in a sumptuous banquet and dance around it, inviting the* **King** *and his party to eat. Then they leave*]

Alonso What harmony is this? My good friends, hark!

Gonzalo Marvellous sweet music!

Alonso Give us kind keepers, heavens! What were these?

Sebastian A living drollery. Now I will believe
That there are unicorns; that in Arabia
There is one tree, the phoenix' throne; one phoenix
At this hour reigning there.

Antonio I'll believe both;
And what does else want credit, come to me,
And I'll be sworn 'tis true: travellers ne'er did lie,
Though fools at home condemn 'em.

Gonzalo If in Naples
I should report this now, would they believe me?
If I should say, I saw such islanders –
For, certes, these are people of the island –
Who, though they are of monstrous shape, yet, note,
Their manners are more gentle, kind, than of
Our human generation you shall find
Many, nay, almost any.

Prospero [*Aside*] Honest lord,
Thou hast said well; for some of you there present
Are worse than devils.

Alonso I cannot too much muse
Such shapes, such gesture, and such sound, expressing –
Although they want the use of tongue – a kind
Of excellent dumb discourse.

Prospero [*Aside*] Praise in departing.

Francisco They vanished strangely.

Sebastian No matter, since
They have left their viands behind; for we have stomachs.
Will 't please you taste of what is here?

Alonso What's this music? Good friends, listen.

Gonzalo Marvelous, sweet music!

Alonso May we be granted guardian angels! What were they?

Sebastian A living puppet show. Now I'll believe in unicorns, and that there's a tree in Arabia especially for the phoenix, on which a phoenix sits right now.

Antonio I'll believe both; and whatever else is incredible, trust me to swear it's true. Travelers never lie, in spite of the fools at home who scorn them!

Gonzalo If I reported this now in Naples, would they believe me? Or if I said I saw such islanders – undoubtedly they *are* natives of this island – and that grotesque though they appeared, they were notably more gentle and kind than many, or indeed any, of us human beings?

Prospero Well said, honest lord. Some of you here are worse than devils.

Alonso I can't stop marveling at the way these strange spirits, with mime and music, are able to communicate so well: a kind of sign language!

Prospero [*aside*] Hold on to your praise till you've seen more!

Francisco They disappeared mysteriously.

Sebastian That doesn't matter. They've left the food behind. We're hungry. [*Deferring to the* **King**] Would you like to try it?

Alonso Not I.

Gonzalo Faith, sir, you need not fear. When we were boys,
Who would believe that there were mountaineers
Dew-lapped like bulls, whose throats had hanging at 'em
Wallets of flesh? or that there were such men
Whose heads stood in their breasts? which now we find
Each putter-out of five for one will bring us
Good warrant of.

Alonso I will stand to, and feed,
Although my last; no matter, since I feel
The best is past. Brother, my lord the duke,
Stand to, and do as we.

[*Thunder and lightning. Enter* **Ariel** *like a Harpy; he claps his wings upon the table; and, with a quaint device, the banquet vanishes*]

Ariel You are three men of sin, whom Destiny –
That hath to instrument this lower world
And what is in 't – the never-surfeited sea
Hath caused to belch up you; and on this island,
Where man doth not inhabit – you 'mongst men
Being most unfit to live. I have made you mad;
And even with such-like valour men hang and drown
Their proper selves.

[**Alonso, Sebastian**, *etc. draw their swords*]

You fools! I and my fellows
Are ministers of Fate: the elements,
Of whom your swords are tempered, may as well
Wound the loud winds, or with bemocked-at stabs
Kill the still-closing waters, as diminish
One dowl that's in my plume: my fellow-ministers
Are like invulnerable. If you could hurt,

Alonso Not I.

Gonzalo Indeed, sir, you needn't worry. When we were children, who would have believed that there were mountain dwellers with pendulous chins like the throats of bulls? Or that there were strange people with no heads and with their eyes and mouths in their chests? Things which every "putter-out of five for one" tells us about nowadays . . . [*A reference to the practice by travelers of buying "insurance" against their return from voyages*]

Alonso I'll buckle down and eat: if it's my last meal it doesn't matter, as I feel I've had the best of my time. Brother, my lord the duke: follow my example and eat.

[*Thunder and lightning.* **Ariel** *enters looking like the fabled Harpy – a foul monster with a woman's face and body, and the wings and claws of a bird. He spreads his wings over the table and the banquet vanishes*]

Ariel You are three sinful men. Providence (that has this world and what is in it as its tool) has made the ever-hungry sea disgorge you upon this uninhabited island, you being of all men the most unfit to live. I have made you mad, and your kind of desperate courage makes men hang and drown themselves.

[**Alonso, Sebastian,** *and the others draw their swords*]

You fools! I and my companions are the ministers of Fate. We are the elements of which your swords are made, so you might as well wound howling gales, kill the ever-closing sea by stabbing it, as try to hurt the smallest feather in my plumage. My fellow spirits are equally invulnerable.

Your swords are now too massy for your strengths,
And will not be uplifted. But remember –
For that's my business to you – that you three
From Milan did supplant good Prospero:
Exposed unto the sea, which hath requit it,
Him and his innocent child: for which foul deed
The powers, delaying, not forgetting, have
Incensed the seas and shores, yea, all the creatures,
Against your peace. Thee of thy son, Alonso,
They have bereft; and do pronounce by me
Ling'ring perdition – worse than any death
Can be at once – shall step by step attend
You and your ways; whose wraths to guard you from –
Which here, in this most desolate isle, else falls
Upon your heads – is nothing but heart-sorrow
And a clear life ensuing.

[*He vanishes in thunder; then, to soft music, enter the Shapes again; they dance, with mocks and mows, carrying out the table*]

Prospero Bravely the figure of this Harpy hast thou
Performed, my Ariel; a grace it had devouring:
Of my instruction hast thou nothing bated
In what thou hadst to say: so, with good life
And observation strange, my meaner ministers
Their several kinds have done. My high charms work,
And these mine enemies are all knit up
In their distractions; they now are in my power;
And in these fits I leave them, while I visit
Young Ferdinand – whom they suppose is drowned –
And his and mine loved darling.

[*Exit*]

Even if you could do hurt, your swords are now too weighty for your strengths; you cannot lift them up. But remember – for this is the purpose of my visit to you – that you three ousted worthy Prospero from Milan, and exposed him and his innocent child to the mercy of the sea. For this foul deed, the gods, postponing but not forgetting, have stirred up the seas, the shores, and every creature against you. They have taken your son away from you, Alonso, and through me they sentence you to lingering suffering, worse than any quick death, which shall be with you always throughout your life. To guard you against their wrath, which will otherwise descend upon you here on this most desolate island, there is no alternative but heartfelt sorrow and a blameless life from now on.

[*He vanishes in a clap of thunder. Then, to soft music, the* **Spirits** *return again and dance mockingly and derisively as they remove the table*]

Prospero You've acted the part of Harpy splendidly, Ariel. It went down very well. You omitted none of my instructions in what you had to say. So also have my lesser servants acted out their various parts in a wonderfully realistic and observant way. My prodigious spells have worked, and all my enemies are totally confused. Now they are in my power. I'll leave them in their disarray, while I visit young Ferdinand, who they think is drowned, and his – and my – beloved.

[*He goes*]

Gonzalo I' th' name of something holy, sir, why stand you
In this strange stare?

Alonso O, it is monstrous, monstrous!
Methought the billows spoke, and told me of it;
The winds did sing it to me; and the thunder,
That deep and dreadful organ-pipe, pronounced
The name of Prosper: it did bass my trespass.
Therefore my son i' th' ooze is bedded; and
I'll seek him deeper than e'er plummet sounded,
And with him there lie mudded.

[*Exit*]

Sebastian But one fiend at a time,
I'll fight their legions o'er.

Antonio I'll be thy second.

[*Exeunt* **Sebastian** *and* **Antonio**]

Gonzalo All three of them are desperate: their great guilt,
Like poison given to work a great time after,
Now 'gins to bite the spirits. I do beseech you,
That are of suppler joints, follow them swiftly,
And hinder them from what this ecstasy
May now provoke them to.

Adrian Follow, I pray you.

[*Exeunt*]

Gonzalo [*to* **Alonso**] In the name of all that's holy, sir, why are you standing there, staring?

Alonso Oh, this is monstrous, monstrous! I thought the waves spoke and told me of my sin. The winds sang it to me. Thunder, like the mournful bass note of an organ, spoke the name "Prospero." It groaned my guilt. And because of it, my son lies in the ooze of the seabed. I'll seek him in the unfathomable depths and join him there in the mud.

[*He goes, distraught*]

Sebastian [*defiantly*] One fiend at a time, I'll fight whole legions of them.

Antonio I'll be your second.

[**Sebastian** *and* **Antonio** *leave*]

Gonzalo All three of them are reckless. Their great guilt, like a slow poison, now starts to bite. I beg you more athletic men to follow them quickly and stop them from doing themselves some injury in their madness.

Adrian [*to the others*] After them, quick!

[*They dash off*]

Act four

Scene 1

Before Prospero's Cell. Enter **Prospero, Ferdinand** *and* **Miranda**

Prospero If I have too austerely punished you,
Your compensation makes amends; for I
Have given you here a third of mine own life,
Or that for which I live; who once again
I tender to thy hand: all thy vexations
Were but trials of thy love, and thou
Hast strangely stood the test: here, afore Heaven,
I ratify this my rich gift. O Ferdinand,
Do not smile at me that I boast her off,
For thou shalt find she will outstrip all praise,
And make it halt behind her.

Ferdinand I do believe it
Against an oracle.

Prospero Then, as my gift, and thine own acquisition
Worthily purchased, take my daughter: but
If thou dost break her virgin-knot before
All sanctimonious ceremonies may
With fully and holy rite be ministered,
No sweet aspersion shall the heavens let fall
To make this contract grow; but barren hate,
Sour-eyed disdain and discord shall bestrew
The union of your bed with weeds so loathly
That you shall hate it both: therefore take heed,
As Hymen's lamps shall light you.

Act four

Scene 1

In front of Prospero's cave. **Prospero, Ferdinand,** *and* **Miranda** *enter.*

Prospero If I've punished you too severely, your compensation [*indicating* **Miranda**] makes amends: I've given you a third of my whole life, or what I live for. Once again I give her to you. All your discomforts were simply my way of testing your love, and you have stood that test wonderfully. Here before Heaven I confirm my priceless gift. Oh, Ferdinand, don't smile when I idolize her: you'll find she is beyond all praise: it can't keep pace with her.

Ferdinand I'd believe it even if an oracle said otherwise!

Prospero So, as my gift and your gain – deservedly won – take my daughter. [*He joins their hands together*] But if you sleep with her before you are properly joined in holy matrimony, your union will be denied the sweet grace of heaven. Barren hate, sour looks of disdain, and conflict will characterize your marriage, so that both of you will loathe it. Take heed, therefore, between now and your wedding day.

Ferdinand As I hope
For quiet days, fair issue and long life,
With such love as 'tis now, the murkiest den,
The most opportune place, the strong'st suggestion
Our worser genius can, shall never melt
Mine honour into lust, to take away
The edge of that day's celebration
When I shall think, or Phoebus' steeds are foundered,
Or Night kept chained below.

Prospero Fairly spoke.
Sit, then, and talk with her; she is thine own.
What, Ariel! My industrious servant, Ariel!

[*Enter* **Ariel**]

Ariel What would my potent master? Here I am.

Prospero Thou and thy meaner fellows your last service
Did worthily perform; and I must use you
In such another trick. Go bring the rabble,
O'er whom I give thee power, here to this place:
Incite them to quick motion; for I must
Bestow upon the eyes of this young couple
Some vanity of mine Art: it is my promise,
And they expect it from me.

Ariel Presently?

Prospero Ay, with a twink.

Ariel Before you can say, 'come' and 'go',
And breathe twice, and cry, 'so, so',
Each one, tripping on his toe,
Will be here with mop and mow.
Do you love me, master? No?

Prospero Dearly, my delicate Ariel. Do not approach
Till thou dost hear me call.

Ferdinand As I hope for peace, a family, and long life, together with enduring love, neither the darkest and most opportune of places, nor the most irresistible of sordid urges will ever turn my honor to lust. It would spoil the enjoyment of our nuptial day, when I'll be thinking that time has stopped and night will never come.

Prospero Well said. Sit and talk to her. She is yours. [*Calling*] Now, Ariel! My hardworking servant, Ariel!

[**Ariel** *enters*]

Ariel What can I do for my all-powerful master? Here I am.

Prospero You and your subordinates played your parts well last time. I want to use you again in a similar illusion. Go and bring here the assistants over whom I have given you authority. Prepare them for a performance. I must let the young couple see another of my magical feats: I promised them and they expect it from me.

Ariel Immediately?

Prospero Yes, in the twinkling of an eye.

Ariel Before you can say "come" and "go," and take two breaths, and cry "yes, yes," they will be here on tiptoe, making their expressive faces. Do you love me, master? Eh?

Prospero Dearly, my delicate Ariel. Don't come here till you hear me call.

Ariel Well, I conceive.

[*Exit*]

Prospero Look thou be true; do not give dalliance
Too much the rein: the strongest oaths are straw
To th' fire i' th' blood: be more abstemious,
Or else, good night your vow!

Ferdinand I warrant you, sir;
The white cold virgin snow upon my heart
Abates the ardour of my liver.

Prospero Well.
Now come, my Ariel! Bring a corollary,
Rather than want a spirit: appear, and pertly!
No tongue! All eyes! Be silent.

[*Soft music*]

[*Enter* **Iris**]

Iris *Ceres, most bounteous lady, thy rich leas*
Of wheat, rye, barley, vetches, oats, and pease;
Thy turfy mountains, where live nibbling sheep,
And flat meads thatched with stover, them to keep;
Thy banks with pioned and twilled brims,
Which spongy April at thy hest betrims,
To make cold nymphs chaste crowns; and thy broom-groves,
Whose shadow the dismissed bachelor loves,
Being lass-lorn; thy poll-clipt vineyard;
And thy sea-marge, sterile and rocky-hard,
Where thou thyself dost air; the queen o' th' sky,
Whose wat'ry arch and messenger am I,
Bids thee leave these; and with her sovereign grace,

Ariel I understand.

[*He goes*]

Prospero [*to* **Ferdinand**] See you keep your word. Don't let your feelings run away with you. Passion is a great destroyer of promises. Exercise more self-control, or else you can say good night to your vow!

Ferdinand I can assure you, sir, that my loved one's snow-white chastity cools my ardor.

Prospero Good. Now, come Ariel! Let's have too many performers rather than too few! Come, and be brisk! No talking! Attention, everybody! Silence!

[*Soft music plays. A masque is performed by the* **Spirits**. *The first appears as* **Iris**, *goddess of the rainbow and messenger of the gods, who addresses* **Ceres**, *goddess of agriculture*]

Iris *Ceres, generous lady, who makes grow*
The cereals and root crops that we sow;
Whose grassy mountains feed the nibbling sheep,
Whose meadows yield the fodder for their keep,
Whose river banks with peonies are dressed,
Which April showers bring – at your request –
For virgins to make crowns of; and your groves
With shadows where the jilted lover roves
All lovesick; and your vineyards, pruned with care,
And your seacoast, so rocky-hard and bare,
Where you yourself will stroll. Queen of the sky,
Juno, whose rainbow messenger am I,
Says leave all these; and with her royal grace –

Here, on this grass-plot, in this very place,
To come and sport; her peacocks fly amain:
Approach, rich Ceres, her to entertain.

[*Enter* **Ceres**]

Ceres *Hail, many-coloured messenger, that ne'er*
Dost disobey the wife of Jupiter;
Who, with thy saffron wings, upon my flowers
Diffusest honey-drops, refreshing showers;
And with each end of thy blue bow dost crown
My bosky acres and my unshrubbed down
Rich scarf to my proud earth, why hath thy queen
Summoned me hither, to this short-grassed green?

Iris *A contract of true love to celebrate;*
And some donation freely to estate
On the blest lovers.

Ceres *Tell me, heavenly bow,*
If Venus or her son, as thou dost know,
Do now attend the queen? Since they did plot
The means that dusky Dis my daughter got,
Her and her blind boy's scandalled company
I have forsworn.

Iris *Of her society*
Be not afraid: I met her deity
Cutting the clouds towards Paphos, and her son
Dove-drawn with her. Here thought they to have done
Some wanton charm upon this man and maid,
Whose vows are, that no bed-right shall be paid
Till Hymen's torch be lighted: but in vain;
Mars's hot minion is returned again;
Her waspish-headed son has broke his arrows,
Swears he will shoot no more, but play with sparrows,
And be a boy right out.

Here, on this grass plot, in this very place –
Join in our fun. In haste her peacocks fly.
To entertain her, Ceres, come and try!

[**Ceres** *enters, played by* **Ariel**]

Ceres *Hail, Iris, rainbow-colored messenger*
Who pleases Juno, wife of Jupiter;
Whose yellow-tinted wings caress my flowers
Dispersing honey drops, refreshing showers;
Each bright end of your blue rainbow crowns
My wooded acres and my barren downs.
Rich ornament of earth, why has your queen
Summoned me here to this trim lawn of green?

Iris *A contract of true love to celebrate,*
And of your bounty, something to donate
To the blest lovers.

Ceres *Tell me, heavenly bow,*
Is Venus or son Cupid, do you know,
Still waiting on the queen? Since that sad day
They helped dark Pluto steal my girl away,
I've vowed to shun their evil company.

Iris *Don't be afraid of her society:*
Up in the sky I met her with her son
Speeding to Paphos. What they thought they'd done
Was this: a spell on man and maid they'd placed –
Who'd vowed that till their marriage they'd be chaste.
It didn't work; the gods had schemed in vain:
Venus, defeated, sped back home again.
Cupid, peevish boy, broke all his arrows;
He swore he'd shoot no more, but play with sparrows,
And be a lad again.

Ceres *Highest queen of state,*
Great Juno comes; I know her by her gait.

[*Enter* **Juno**]

Juno *How does my bounteous sister? Go with me*
To bless this twain, that they may prosperous be,
And honoured in their issue.

[*Singing*]
Honour, riches, marriage-blessing,
Long continuance, and increasing,
Hourly joys be still upon you!
Juno sings her blessings on you.

Ceres [*Singing*]
Earth's increase, and foison plenty,
Barns and garners never empty;
Vines with clust'ring bunches growing;
Plants with goodly burthen bowing;
Spring come to you at the farthest
In the very end of harvest!
Scarcity and want shall shun you;
Ceres' blessing so is on you.

Ferdinand This is a most majestic vision, and
Harmonious charmingly. May I be bold
To think these spirits?

Prospero Spirits, which by mine Art
I have from their confines called to enact
My present fancies.

Ferdinand Let me live here ever;
So rare a wondered father and a wise
Makes this place a Paradise.

[**Juno** *and* **Ceres** *whisper, and send* **Iris** *on employment*]

Ceres *Highest queen of state,*
Great Juno comes. I know her by her gait.

[**Juno** *enters*]

Juno *How is my bounteous sister? Come with me*
To bless these two, that they may prosperous be
And honored in their children.

[*singing*]
Honor, riches, marriage blessing,
Long continuance, and increasing,
Hourly joys be always with you!
Juno sings her blessings on you.

Ceres [*singing*]
Ample crops and harvests plenty,
Barns and haylofts never empty;
Vines with massive bunches growing;
Plants with heavy burdens bowing;
Spring comes to you at the farthest
At the very end of harvest!
Scarcity and want shall shun you;
Ceres' blessing so is on you.

Ferdinand This is a most majestic spectacle; its theme of universal harmony is spellbinding. Do I take it these are spirits?

Prospero [*nodding*] Spirits that I have summoned from their confines by means of my magic art to do my bidding.

Ferdinand Let me live here forever; so wise a father-in-law, capable of working such wonders, makes this place a paradise.

[**Juno** *and* **Ceres** *whisper and send* **Iris** *away to perform a task*]

Prospero Sweet, now, silence!
Juno and Ceres whisper seriously;
There's something else to do: hush, and be mute,
Or else our spell is marred.

Iris *You nymphs, called Naiads, of the wind'ring brooks,*
With your sedged crowns and ever-harmless looks,
Leave your crisp channels, and on this green land
Answer your summons; Juno does command:
Come, temperate nymphs, and help to celebrate
A contract of true love; be not too late.

[*Enter certain* **Nymphs**]

You sunburned sicklemen, of August weary,
Come hither from the furrow, and be merry:
Make holiday; your rye-straw hats put on,
And these fresh nymphs encounter every one
In country footing.

[*Enter certain* **Reapers**, *properly habited. They join with the* **Nymphs** *in a graceful dance; towards the end whereof* **Prospero** *starts suddenly, and speaks; after which, to a strange, hollow, and confused noise, they heavily vanish*]

Prospero [*Aside*] I had forgot that foul conspiracy
Of the beast Caliban and his confederates
Against my life: the minute of their plot
Is almost come. [*To the* **Spirits**] Well done! Avoid, no more!

Ferdinand This is strange: your father's in some passion
That works him strongly.

Miranda Never till this day
Saw I him touched with anger, so distempered.

Prospero You do look, my son, in a moved sort,
As if you were dismayed: be cheerful, sir.

Prospero Ssh, now! Silence! Juno and Ceres are whispering earnestly: there's more to come. Hush, and say no more, or else the spell will be broken.

Iris *You nymphs, called "Naiads," of meandering brooks,*
With your reedy crowns and ever-harmless looks,
Leave your rippling streams, and on this green land
Answer your summons: it's Juno's command.
Come, mild-mannered nymphs; help to celebrate
A contract of true love: so don't be late.

[*Several* **Nymphs** *enter*]

You sunburnt harvesters, of August weary,
Come in from your reaping and be merry:
Make holiday; your rye-straw hats put on,
And take the nymphs as partners, every one,
In country dancing.

[*A group of* **Reapers** *enters, finely dressed. They join in a graceful dance with the* **Nymphs**. *Toward the end,* **Prospero** *suddenly gives a start and speaks. The dancers sorrowfully vanish, accompanied by strange, hollow, and confused noises*]

Prospero [*aside*] I'd forgotten the foul plot against my life of that bestial Caliban and his fellow-conspirators. They'll be here any minute. [*To the* **Spirits**] Well done! Begone! No more!

Ferdinand This is odd. Your father's worked up about something.

Miranda I've never seen him so angry, so out of temper.

Prospero [*controlling himself, and seeing that* **Ferdinand** *is distressed*] You look worried, my son, and ill at ease. Cheer up, sir, our entertainment is over. Our actors, as I said

Our revels now are ended. These our actors,
As I foretold you, were all spirits, and
Are melted into air, into thin air:
And, like the baseless fabric of this vision,
The cloud-capped towers, the gorgeous palaces,
The solemn temples, the great globe itself,
Yea, all which it inherit, shall dissolve,
And, like this insubstantial pageant faded,
Leave not a rack behind. We are such stuff
As dreams are made on; and our little life
Is rounded with a sleep. Sir, I am vexed;
Bear with my weakness; my old brain is troubled:
Be not disturbed with my infirmity:
If you be pleased, retire into my cell,
And there repose: a turn or two I'll walk,
To still my beating mind.

Ferdinand
Miranda We wish your peace.

[*Exeunt*]

Prospero Come with a thought. I thank thee: Ariel, come.

[*Enter* **Ariel**]

Ariel Thy thoughts I cleave to. What's thy pleasure?

Prospero Spirit,
We must prepare to meet with Caliban.

Ariel Ay, my commander: when I presented Ceres,
I thought to have told thee of it; but I feared
Lest I might anger thee.

Prospero Say again, where didst thou leave these varlets?

Ariel I told you, sir, they were red-hot with drinking;

before, were all spirits, and have melted into air, thin air. And just as this was all an illusion, so lofty towers, gorgeous palaces, solemn temples, the earth itself, and all, indeed, who live on it, will disappear; and just as this insubstantial performance faded away, likewise not even a cloud will be left behind. We are made of the same stuff as dreams, and our short lives are rounded off with a sleep. Sir, I'm angry. Bear with my weakness. My old brain is troubled. Don't be disturbed by my infirmity. Perhaps you'd retire to my cave and rest there. I'll take a stroll to calm my overactive mind.

Ferdinand
Miranda May you find peace.

[*They go*]

Prospero I summon you in my thoughts. Thank you, Ariel! Come!

[**Ariel** *enters*]

Ariel I'm tuned to your thinking. What can I do for you?

Prospero Spirit, we must get ready to deal with Caliban.

Ariel Indeed, my commander. When I acted the part of Ceres, it occurred to me to remind you about it, but I was afraid to anger you with the interruption.

Prospero Tell me again: where did you leave those rogues?

Ariel I told you, sir. They were rip-roaring drunk: so full of

So full of valour that they smote the air
For breathing in their faces; beat the ground
For kissing of their feet; yet always bending
Towards their project. Then I beat my tabor;
At which, like unbacked colts, they pricked their ears,
Advanced their eyelids, lifted up their noses
As they smelt music: so I charmed their ears,
That, calf-like, they my lowing followed, through
Toothed briers, sharp furzes, pricking goss, and thorns,
Which entered their frail shins: at last I left them
I' th' filthy-mantled pool beyond your cell,
There dancing up to th' chins, that the foul lake
O'erstunk their feet.

Prospero This was well done, my bird.
Thy shape invisible retain thou still:
The trumpery in my house, go bring it hither,
For stale to catch these thieves.

Ariel I go, I go.

Prospero A devil, a born devil, on whose nature
Nurture can never stick; on whom my pains,
Humanely taken, all, all lost, quite lost;
And as with age his body uglier grows,
So his mind cankers. I will plague them all,
Even to roaring.

[*Enter* **Ariel**, *loaden with glistering apparel, etc.*]

Come, hang them on this line.

[**Prospero** *and* **Ariel** *remain, invisible*]

[*Enter* **Caliban, Stephano,** *and* **Trinculo**, *all wet*]

Caliban Pray you, tread softly, that the blind mole may not
Hear a foot fall: we now are near his cell.

Dutch courage that they struck the air for breathing in their faces, beat the ground for kissing their feet – but always making toward their objective. Then I beat my drum, at which, like unbroken colts, they pricked up their ears, raised their eyelids, and flared their nostrils as they smelt the music. So I put a spell on their ears, which made them follow my sounds like calves: through spiky briers, sharp bracken, prickly gorse, and thorns which stuck in their delicate shins. Finally I left them in the pool that's covered with green scum on the far side of your cave, bobbing about up to their chins, making the lake stink more than their feet.

Prospero You've done well, my bird. Keep your invisibility a little longer. Go and bring some trivial articles from my house to act as bait for catching these thieves.

Ariel I go, I go . . .

[*He leaves*]

Prospero [*musing about* **Caliban**] He's a devil, a born devil, whose nature can't be permanently changed by a civilized upbringing; on whom the trouble I took for humane reasons has been all wasted, utterly wasted. As he grows uglier with age, so correspondingly his mind gets fouler. I'll make them all suffer till they scream!

[**Ariel** *enters, carrying glittering clothes and eye-catching accessories*]

Come, hang them on this line.

[*They spread them out and step back, both invisible*]

[**Caliban, Stephano,** *and* **Trinculo** *enter, very wet*]

Caliban Please now: walk quietly so that even a blind mole can't hear your footstep. We're near his cave.

Stephano Monster, your fairy, which you say is a harmless fairy, has done little better than played the Jack with us.

Trinculo Monster, I do smell all horse-piss; at which my nose is in great indignation.

Stephano So is mine. Do you hear, monster? If I should take a displeasure against you, look you –

Trinculo Thou wert but a lost monster.

Caliban Good my lord, give me thy favour still.
Be patient, for the prize I'll bring thee to
Shall hoodwink this mischance: therefore speak softly.
All's hushed as midnight yet.

Trinculo Ay, but to lose our bottles in the pool!

Stephano There is not only disgrace and dishonour in that, monster, but an infinite loss.

Trinculo That's more to me than my wetting: yet this is your harmless fairy, monster.

Stephano I will fetch off my bottle, though I be o'er ears for my labour.

Caliban Prithee, my King, be quiet. See'st thou here,
This is the mouth o' th' cell: no noise, and enter.
Do that good mischief which may make this island
Thine own for ever, and I, thy Caliban,
For aye thy foot-licker.

Stephano Give me thy hand. I do begin to have bloody thoughts.

Trinculo O King Stephano! O peer! O worthy Stephano!
Look what a wardrobe here is for thee!

Caliban Let it alone, thou fool; it is but trash.

Stephano Monster, your fairy – which you said was a harmless fairy – has done little more than play the fool with us . . .

Trinculo Monster, I smell like horse urine, which greatly offends my nose.

Stephano So do I. Do you hear, monster? If I should take a sudden dislike to you, you know –

Trinculo You'd be an ex-monster.

Caliban My lord, do not reject me. Be patient, because the prize I'll bring you will blot out this mishap. So lower your voice. All's as silent as the night.

Trinculo Yes, but to lose our bottles in the pool –

Stephano That's not only disgraceful and dishonorable, monster, but also an infinite loss.

Trinculo That means more to me than my wetting: yet this is your ''harmless'' fairy, monster!

Stephano I'll recover my bottle even if I am drowned for my trouble.

Caliban Please, my king, be quiet. Look here – this is the mouth of the cave. Make no noise and enter. Do that good deed of mischief which will make this island your own forever, and I – your Caliban – your eternal foot-licker.

Stephano Give me your hand. I begin to have thoughts of blood!

Trinculo [*noticing the fancy clothes on display*] Oh, King Stephano! Oh, lord! Oh, worthy Stephano! Look what a wardrobe there is for you here!

Caliban Leave it alone, you fool. It's only trash.

Trinculo O, ho, monster! We know what belongs to a frippery. O King Stephano!

Stephano Put off that gown, Trinculo; by this hand, I'll have that gown.

Trinculo Thy grace shall have it.

Caliban The dropsy drown this fool! What do you mean
To dote thus on such luggage? Let't alone,
And do the murder first: if he awake,
From toe to crown he'll fill our skins with pinches,
Make us strange stuff.

Stephano Be you quiet, monster. Mistress line, is not this my jerkin? Now is the jerkin under the line: now, jerkin, you are like to lose your hair, and prove a bald jerkin.

Trinculo Do, do; we steal by line and level, an't like your grace.

Stephano I thank thee for that jest; here's a garment for't: wit shall not go unrewarded while I am King of this country. 'Steal by line and level' is an excellent pass of pate; there's another garment for't.

Trinculo Monster, come, put some lime upon your fingers, and away with the rest.

Caliban I will have none on't: we shall lose our time,
And all be turned to barnacles, or to apes
With foreheads villainous low.

Stephano Monster, lay-to your fingers: help to bear this away where my hogshead of wine is, or I'll turn you out of my kingdom: go to, carry this.

Trinculo [*trying on a garment*] Oh ho, monster! We know what belongs to a secondhand shop! Oh, King Stephano! [*He parades around in his finery*]

Stephano Take off that cloak, Trinculo. By god, *I'll* have that cloak!

Trinculo [*bowing*] Your Grace shall have it. [*He hands it over*]

Caliban May the fool drop dead! What's the idea of drooling over fancy clothes? Leave them alone, and do the murder first. If he wakes up he'll pinch us all over from head to toe and tear us to ribbons.

Stephano Be quiet, you monster! [*Strutting around in an elaborate jacket, and talking to the clothesline*] Madam Line, don't you think this jacket suits me? [*He strokes the fur trimming*] But since it's not a quality line, it will likely lose its hair and go bald.

Trinculo It will, it will. We should do our level best to steal a quality line, so please Your Grace.

Stephano Thanks for that witticism: here's a garment for it. [*He gives* **Trinculo** *a gift from the clothesline*] Wit will not go unrewarded while I'm king of this country. "Do our level best to steal a quality line" is an excellent wisecrack. There's another for it. [*In lordly fashion, he bestows another garment on* **Trinculo**]

Trinculo Monster, come on. Put some glue on your fingers and steal the rest.

Caliban I'll have nothing to do with it. We'll miss our opportunity, and we'll all be turned into wild geese or to apes with villainously low foreheads.

Stephano Monster, put your fingers to good use, and help to carry all this away to where my barrel of wine is, or I'll turn you out of my kingdom. Go on [*piling clothes on him*] – carry this.

Trinculo And this.

Stephano Ay, and this.

[*A noise of hunters is heard. Enter divers* **Spirits,** *in shape of dogs and hounds, hunting them about;* **Prospero** *and* **Ariel** *set them on*]

Prospero Hey, Mountain, hey!

Ariel Silver! there it goes, Silver!

Prospero Fury, Fury! there, Tyrant, there! hark, hark!

[**Caliban, Stephano** *and* **Trinculo** *are driven out*]

Go charge my goblins that they grind their joints
With dry convulsions; shorten up their sinews
With aged cramps; and more pinch-spotted make them
Than pard or cat o' mountain.

Ariel Hark, they roar!

Prospero Let them be hunted soundly. At this hour
Lies at my mercy all mine enemies:
Shortly shall all my labours end, and thou
Shalt have the air at freedom: for a little
Follow, and do me service.

[*Exeunt*]

Trinculo And this . . .

Stephano Yes, and this . . .

[*A noise of hunting is heard. Several* **Spirits** *enter, disguised as hounds. They chase* **Stephano, Trinculo,** *and* **Caliban,** *encouraged by* **Prospero** *and* **Ariel,** *who address the* **Spirits** *individually by name, like hunting dogs*]

Prospero Hey, Mountain, hey!

Ariel Silver! There it goes, Silver!

Prospero Fury, Fury! There, Tyrant, there! Listen, listen!

[**Stephano, Trinculo,** *and* **Caliban** *are chased away*]

Order my goblins to grind their joints with painful seizures, tighten their muscles with long-lasting cramps, and pinch their skins till they're more blotched than panthers or leopards!

Ariel Listen to them roar!

Prospero Let them be well and truly hounded. At this point in time, all my enemies are at my mercy. Soon all my labors will be at an end, and you shall be as free as air. For a little while longer, follow my instructions and stay in my service.

[*They go*]

Act five

Scene 1

Before the Cell of Prospero. Enter **Prospero** *in his magic robes, and* **Ariel**

Prospero Now does my project gather to a head:
My charms crack not; my spirits obey; and time
Goes upright with his carriage. How's the day?

Ariel On the sixth hour; at which time, my lord,
You said our work should cease.

Prospero I did say so,
When first I raised the tempest. Say, my spirit,
How fares the King and 's followers?

Ariel Confined together
In the same fashion as you gave in charge,
Just as you left them; all prisoners, sir,
In the lime-grove which weather-fends your cell;
They cannot budge till your release. The King,
His brother, and yours, abide all three distracted,
And the remainder mourning over them,
Brimful of sorrow and dismay; but chiefly
Him you termed, sir, 'The good old lord, Gonzalo';
His tears run down his beard, like winter's drops
From eaves of reeds. Your charm so strongly works 'em,
That if you now beheld them, your affections
Would become tender.

Prospero Dost thou think so, spirit?

Ariel Mine would, sir, were I human.

Act five

Scene 1

In front of **Prospero***'s cave, a little later.* **Prospero** *enters in his magic robes, followed by* **Ariel**.

Prospero Now my scheme is coming to a climax. My spells hold together; my spirits obey; everything is running according to schedule. What time is it?

Ariel Six o'clock: the time you said our work would finish.

Prospero I did say that when I first stirred up the tempest. Tell me, my spirit, how are the king and his followers?

Ariel Kept together as you instructed, just as you left them. They're all prisoners in the lime grove which protects your cave from the weather. They can't budge till you release them. The king, his brother, and your brother are distressed, all three of them, with the rest mourning over them, brimful of sorrow and dismay. Most affected is the one you called "The good old lord, Gonzalo." His tears run down his beard like winter rain from a thatched roof. They are so spellbound that if you saw them now, your feelings would be touched.

Prospero Do you think so, spirit?

Ariel Mine would be, sir, if I were human.

Prospero And mine shall.
Hast thou, which art but air, a touch, a feeling
Of their afflictions, and shall not myself,
One of their kind, that relish all as sharply,
Passion as they, be kindlier moved than thou art?
Though with their high wrongs I am struck to th' quick,
Yet with my nobler reason 'gainst my fury
Do I take part: the rarer action is
In virtue than in vengeance: they being penitent,
The sole drift of my purpose doth extend
Not a frown further. Go release them, Ariel:
My charms I'll break, their senses I'll restore,
And they shall be themselves.

Ariel I'll fetch them, sir.

[*Exit*]

Prospero Ye elves of hills, brooks, standing lakes, and groves;
And ye that on the sands with printless foot
Do chase the ebbing Neptune, and do fly him
When he comes back; you demi-puppets that
By moonshine do the green sour ringlets make,
Whereof the ewe not bites; and you whose pastime
Is to make midnight mushrooms, that rejoice
To hear the solemn curfew; by whose aid –
Weak masters though ye be – I have bedimmed
The noontide sun, called forth the mutinous winds,
And 'twixt the green sea and the azured vault
Set roaring war: to the dread rattling thunder
Have I given fire, and rifted Jove's stout oak
With his own bolt; the strong-based promontory
Have I made shake, and by the spurs plucked up
The pine and cedar: graves at my command
Have waked their sleepers, oped, and let 'em forth
By my so potent Art. But this rough magic

Prospero So shall mine. If you, mere air, can experience a sympathy for them in their suffering, then surely I – one of their own kind, with emotions identical to theirs – must be more compassionate than you are? Though I'm deeply hurt by their injustices to me, I control my anger by favoring that nobler quality, reason. Forgiveness is of a higher order than vengeance. If they repent, then I've achieved my purpose. Go and release them, Ariel. I'll break my spells, restore their senses, and they'll be themselves again.

Ariel I'll fetch them, sir.

[*He goes*]

Prospero You elves of hills, brooks, calm lakes, and groves! And you light-footed spirits that chase the ocean when it ebbs, and run away from it when it flows back! You fairies who make rings on village greens by moonlight, so sour that ewes won't crop the grass! And you whose pastime is to make the mushrooms grow at midnight, and who like to hear the solemn curfew bell! With your aid, lesser spirits though you are, I have dimmed the sun at noon, summoned violent storms, and made the green sea and the blue sky wage roaring war. I have added fireballs to fearful, booming thunder, and split stout oaks – Jove's sacred trees – with his own thunderbolts. I've shaken rock-solid headlands, and plucked up pines and cedars by the roots. At my command, graves have awakened those sleeping within, opened up, and let them out, through my so powerful art. But this crude

I here abjure; and, when I have required
Some heavenly music – which even now I do –
To work mine end upon their senses, that
This airy charm is for, I'll break my staff,
Bury it certain fathoms in the earth,
And deeper than did ever plummet sound
I'll drown my book.

[*Solemn music*]

[*Here enters* **Ariel** *before: then* **Alonso**, *with a frantic gesture attended by* **Gonzalo; Sebastian** *and* **Antonio** *in like manner, attended by* **Adrian** *and* **Francisco**. *They all enter the circle which* **Prospero** *had made, and there stand charmed; which* **Prospero** *observing, speaks:*]

A solemn air, and the best comforter
To an unsettled fancy, cure thy brains,
Now useless, boiled within thy skull! There stand,
For you are spell-stopped.
Holy Gonzalo, honourable man,
Mine eyes, ev'n sociable to the show of thine,
Fall fellowly drops. The charm dissolves apace;
And as the morning steals upon the night,
Melting the darkness, so their rising senses
Begin to chase the ignorant fumes that mantle
Their clearer reason. O good Gonzalo,
My true preserver, and a loyal sir
To him thou follow'st! I will pay thy graces
Home both in word and deed. Most cruelly
Didst thou, Alonso, use me and my daughter:
Thy brother was a furtherer in the act.
Thou art pinched for't now, Sebastian. Flesh and blood,
You, brother mine, that entertained ambition,
Expelled remorse and nature; whom, with Sebastian –
Whose inward pinches therefore are most strong –
Would here have killed your King; I do forgive thee,

kind of magic I now renounce, and when I have requested some heavenly music – which I do now – to charm their senses, I'll snap my wand in two, bury it in the earth at the prescribed depth, and drown my magician's book in the unfathomable depths of the ocean.

[*Solemn music is played.* **Ariel** *enters, followed by* **Alonso,** *who is gesturing wildly, like a man who has lost his wits;* **Gonzalo** *is looking after him.* **Sebastian** *and* **Antonio** *also act demented and are being cared for by* **Adrian** *and* **Francisco.** *They all enter* **Prospero's** *magic circle and stand there, spellbound.* **Prospero** *addresses them*]

[*To* **Alonso**] Let solemn music, so soothing to a mind disturbed, cure the distracted brain that lies so useless in your skull! [*To the whole group*] Stand there: you are paralyzed with a spell. Saintly Gonzalo, you honorable man, my eyes shed tears of fellowship in sympathy with yours. The spell quickly fades, and just as morning overtakes night, dispelling darkness, so their reviving senses disperse the ignorance that befogs their brains. Oh, good Gonzalo, my savior and a loyal follower of your lord! I will amply reward your virtuous services, both in word and deed. Alonso, you most cruelly mistreated me and my daughter: your brother acted as your accomplice. You are conscience-stricken now, Sebastian! [*To* **Antonio**] You, my brother, my own flesh and blood, who allowed ambition to be a substitute for compassion and fraternal feelings, and who, with Sebastian – whose pangs of conscience are therefore very strong – would have killed your king here: I forgive you, unnatural

Unnatural though thou art. Their understanding
Begins to swell; and the approaching tide
Will shortly fill the reasonable shore,
That now lies foul and muddy. Not one of them
That yet looks on me, or would know me: Ariel,
Fetch me the hat and rapier in my cell:
I will discase me, and myself present
As I was sometime Milan: quickly, spirit;
Thou shalt ere long be free.

[**Ariel** *sings and helps to attire him*]

Where the bee sucks, there suck I;
In a cowslip's bell I lie;
There I couch when owls do cry.
On the bat's back I do fly
After summer merrily.
Merrily, merrily shall I live now
Under the blossom that hangs on the bough.

Prospero Why, that's my dainty Ariel! I shall miss thee;
But yet thou shalt have freedom: so, so, so.
To the King's ship, invisible as thou art:
There shalt thou find the mariners asleep
Under the hatches; the master and the boatswain
Being awake, enforce them to this place,
And presently, I prithee.

Ariel I drink the air before me, and return
Or ere your pulse twice beat.

Gonzalo All torment, trouble, wonder and amazement
Inhabits here: some heavenly power guide us
Our of this fearful country!

Prospero Behold, Sir King,
The wronged Duke of Milan, Prospero:

though you are. [**Gonzalo, Alonso, Sebastian,** *and* **Antonio** *are gradually shedding the effects of the spell*] Their understanding is beginning to flood back; soon what's now obscure will be quite clear. None of them can see me yet, or would know me if he could see. Ariel, fetch me the hat and rapier from my cell. I'll remove my robe, and present myself as the duke of Milan. Quickly, spirit! You'll be free soon.

[**Ariel** *sings as he helps to dress* **Prospero** *in his robes*]

Where the bee sucks, there suck I:
In a cowslip's bell I lie;
There I sleep when owls do cry.
On the bat's back I do fly
After summer, merrily.
Merrily, merrily shall I live now
Under the blossom that hangs on the bough.

Prospero Why, that's my dainty Ariel! I shall miss you, but you shall have your freedom. [*He arranges his ducal clothes and accessories so as to look his best*] There, there, there. [*To* **Ariel** *again*] Go to the king's ship, invisibly. There you'll find the sailors asleep under the hatches. When the bosun and captain are properly awake, make them come here, and quickly please.

Ariel I'll streak through space, and return before your pulse can beat twice.

[*He goes*]

Gonzalo This place is all torment, trouble, strangeness, and bewilderment. May divine guidance lead us from this dreadful country!

Prospero [*confronting* **Alonso**] See, Sir King, the wronged duke of Milan – Prospero! To confirm that a living prince is

For more assurance that a living Prince
Does now speak to thee, I embrace thy body;
And to thee and thy company I bid
A hearty welcome.

Alonso Whether thou be'st he or no,
Or some enchanted trifle to abuse me,
As late I have been, I not know: thy pulse
Beats, as of flesh and blood; and, since I saw thee,
Th' affliction of my mind amends, with which,
I fear, a madness held me: this must crave –
An if this be at all – a most strange story.
Thy dukedom I resign, and do entreat
Thou pardon me my wrongs. But how should Prospero
Be living and be here?

Prospero First, noble friend
Let me embrace thine age, whose honour cannot
Be measured or confined.

Gonzalo Whether this be
Or be not, I'll not swear.

Prospero You do yet taste
Some subtleties o' the isle, that will not let you
Believe things certain. Welcome, my friends all!
[*Aside to* **Sebastian** *and* **Antonio**] But you, my brace of lords, were I so minded,
I here could pluck his highness' frown upon you,
And justify you traitors: at this time
I will tell no tales.

Sebastian [*Aside*] The devil speaks in him.

Prospero No.
For you, most wicked sir, whom to call brother
Would even infect my mouth, I do forgive
Thy rankest fault – all of them; and require

indeed speaking to you, I embrace you. [*He holds* **Alonso** *to him*] To you and your company I bid a hearty welcome.

Alonso Whether you are Prospero or not, or some kind of magic trick like the others that have deluded me recently, I don't know. Your pulse beats like a normal man's. Since seeing you, the madness is cured from which, I fear, I have suffered. If this is all real, it's part of a most remarkable story. I will no longer extort tribute money: and I beg you to pardon the wrongs I have done you. But how can Prospero be alive and living here?

Prospero [*turning to* **Gonzalo**] First, noble friend, let me embrace your old self. Your honor is beyond measure or limit.

Gonzalo [*dazed*] Whether this is really happening or not, I can't say.

Prospero You are still influenced by the island's magical qualities, which stops you from believing in realities. Welcome, my friends, one and all! [*Aside to* **Sebastian** *and* **Antonio**] But you, my fine pair of lords, if I were so inclined I could expose you before the king and prove you are traitors. Right now, I'll tell no tales. . . .

Sebastian [*aside*] It's the devil speaking!

Prospero No! [*To* **Antonio**] As for you, you wicked man, whom to call "brother" would soil my mouth, I forgive the foulest of your deeds. Nay, all of them. I require my

My dukedom of thee, which perforce, I know,
Thou must restore.

Alonso If thou be'st Prospero,
Give us particulars of thy preservation;
How thou hast met us here, whom three hours since
Were wracked upon this shore; where I have lost –
How sharp the point of this remembrance is! –
My dear son Ferdinand.

Prospero I am woe for't, sir.

Alonso Irreparable is the loss; and patience
Says it is past her cure.

Prospero I rather think
You have not sought her help, of whose soft grace
For the like loss I have her sovereign aid,
And rest myself content.

Alonso You the like loss!

Prospero As great to me, as late; and, supportable
To make the dear loss, have I means much weaker
Than you may call to comfort you, for I
Have lost my daughter.

Alonso A daughter?
O heavens, that they were living both in Naples,
The King and Queen there! That they were, I wish
Myself were mudded in that oozy bed
Where my son lies. When did you lose your daughter?

Prospero In this last tempest. I perceive, these lords
At this encounter do so much admire,
That they devour their reason, and scarce think
Their eyes do offices of truth, their words
Are natural breath: but, howsoe'er you have
Been justled from your senses, know for certain

dukedom from you, which I know you have no alternative but to give back.

Alonso If you are Prospero, explain how you came to be saved, and how you met us here, where three hours ago we were shipwrecked, and where I lost – how keenly I feel the memory of it! – my dear son Ferdinand.

Prospero I am sorry about that, sir.

Alonso The loss is irreparable. Even Patience cannot remedy it.

Prospero I suspect you have not sought her help. I have her supreme aid in a similar loss, thanks to her gentle mercy, and I am reconciled to it.

Alonso You, a similar loss?

Prospero As great to me, and as recent. And to bear the great loss, I have less to sustain me than you can call upon for comfort, because I have lost my daughter. [*He means, of course, that she is engaged to be married*]

Alonso A daughter? Oh, if only they were both living in Naples, as king and queen! If that could be, I'd wish myself buried in the oozy mud of the seabed, where my son lies. When did you lose your daughter?

Prospero In this recent tempest . . . [*He changes the subject*] I see these lords are openmouthed in astonishment at this encounter; they can't believe their eyes; they're speechless.

That I am Prospero, and that very duke
Which was thrust forth of Milan; who most strangely
Upon this shore, where you were wracked, was landed,
To be the lord on't. No more yet of this;
For 'tis a chronicle of day by day,
Not a relation for a breakfast, nor
Befitting this first meeting. Welcome, sir;
This cell's my court: here have I few attendants,
And subjects none abroad: pray you, look in.
My dukedom since you have given me again,
I will requite you with as good a thing;
At least bring forth a wonder, to content ye
As much as me my dukedom.

[*Here* **Prospero** *discovers* **Ferdinand** *and* **Miranda** *playing at chess*]

Miranda Sweet lord, you play me false.

Ferdinand No, my dearest love,
I would not for the world.

Miranda Yes, for a score of kingdoms you should wrangle,
And I would call it fair play.

Alonso If this prove
A vision of the island, one dear son
Shall I twice lose.

Sebastian A most high miracle!

Ferdinand Though the seas threaten, they are merciful;
I have cursed them without cause.

Alonso Now all the blessings
Of a glad father compass thee about!
Arise, and say how thou cam'st here.

However surprising it may be to you, I am assuredly Prospero, the selfsame duke who was expelled from Milan, and who, strange as it may seem, was landed on this shore where you were wrecked, to be the lord of the island. That's enough for now: it's a story requiring days, not one to be told over breakfast or befitting our first meeting. Welcome, sir. This cave is my court. Here, I have few servants and no subjects elsewhere. Please look around inside. Since you have given me my dukedom back, I'll reciprocate with something just as good: a miracle, no less, to please you as much as my dukedom does me.

[**Prospero** *reveals* **Ferdinand** *and* **Miranda** *inside the cave, playing chess*]

Miranda Sweetheart: you're cheating!

Ferdinand No, darling, I wouldn't do that for the world.

Miranda You would! And even if the stake were only a score of kingdoms, I'd call that fair play!

Alonso If this is only another illusion, I'll have lost my dear son twice.

Sebastian A miracle from on high!

Ferdinand [*to Alonso*] Though the seas seem dangerous, they are merciful. I have cursed them without good cause.

Alonso [*to* **Ferdinand**, *who has fallen on his knees*] Now all the blessings of a happy father protect you always! Arise, and tell me how you came here.

Miranda O, wonder!
How many goodly creatures are there here!
How beauteous mankind is! O brave new world,
That has such people in it!

Prospero 'Tis new to thee.

Alonso What is this maid with whom thou wast at play?
Your eld'st acquaintance cannot be three hours:
Is she the goddess that hath severed us,
And brought us thus together?

Ferdinand Sir, she is mortal;
But by immortal Providence she's mine:
I chose her when I could not ask my father
For his advice, nor thought I had one. She
Is daughter to this famous Duke of Milan,
Of whom so often I have heard renown,
But never saw before; of whom I have
Received a second life; and second father
This lady makes him to me.

Alonso I am hers:
But, O, how oddly will it sound that I
Must ask my child forgiveness!

Prospero There, sir, stop:
Let us not burthen our remembrances with
A heaviness that's gone.

Gonzalo I have inly wept,
Or should have spoke ere this. Look down, you gods,
And on this couple drop a blessed crown!
For it is you that have chalked forth the way
Which brought us hither.

Alonso I say, Amen, Gonzalo!

Miranda [*staring in amazement at the company around the cave*] Oh, how wonderful! How many fine people there are here! How lovely mankind is! Oh, what a fabulous new world, that has such people in it!

Prospero It's new to you.

Alonso [*to* **Ferdinand**] Who is the young lady with whom you were playing chess? You can only have known her for three hours. Is she the goddess who parted us and now has brought us together again?

Ferdinand Sir, she is mortal. By the grace of God, she's mine. I chose her when I couldn't ask my father for advice, nor thought I had one. She is the daughter of this famous duke of Milan [*indicating* **Prospero**] of whom I've often heard but never seen, and by whom I have been given a second life. This lady [*indicating* **Miranda**] makes him my father-in-law.

Alonso And equally, I am hers. But how strange it will sound for me to ask my child for forgiveness!

Prospero Stop there, sir. Don't let's stir up memories of sorrows past.

Gonzalo I've been weeping to myself, or I'd have spoken before now. May the gods take note and grant this couple a blessed crown: because [*turning to* **Ferdinand** *and* **Miranda**] it is you two who have pioneered the path that has brought us here.

Alonso Amen to that, Gonzalo!

Gonzalo Was Milan thrust from Milan, that his issue
Should become Kings of Naples? O, rejoice
Beyond a common joy! And set it down
With gold on lasting pillars: in one voyage
Did Claribel her husband find at Tunis;
And Ferdinand, her brother, found a wife
Where he himself was lost; Prospero his dukedom
In a poor isle; and all of us ourselves
When no man was his own.

Alonso [*To* **Ferdinand** *and* **Miranda**] Give me your hands:
Let grief and sorrow still embrace his heart
That doth not wish you joy!

Gonzalo Be it so! Amen!

[*Enter* **Ariel** *with the* **Master** *and* **Boatswain** *amazedly following*]

O, look, sir, look, sir! Here is more of us:
I prophesied, if a gallows were on land,
This fellow could not drown. Now, blasphemy,
That swear'st grace o'erboard, not an oath on shore?
Hast thou no mouth by land? What is the news?

Boatswain The best news is, that we have safely found
Our King, and company; the next, our ship –
Which, but three glasses since, we gave out split –
Is tight and yare and bravely rigged, as when
We first put out to sea.

Ariel [*Aside to* **Prospero**] Sir, all this service
Have I done since I went.

Prospero [*Aside to* **Ariel**] My tricksy spirit!

Alonso These are not natural events; they strengthen
From strange to stranger. Say, how came you hither?

Gonzalo Was the duke of Milan expelled from Milan so that his grandson should be king of Naples? Oh, such extraordinary happiness! Inscribe it in gold on granite pillars: "On one voyage, Claribel found a husband in Tunis; Ferdinand, her brother, found a wife when he himself was lost; Prospero found his dukedom on a poor island; and all of us found ourselves when we were all misguided."

Alonso [*to* **Ferdinand** *and* **Miranda**] Give me your hands. May he who does not wish you joy suffer grief and sorrow evermore!

Gonzalo So be it! Amen!

[**Ariel** *returns with the* **Captain** *and* **Bosun**, *both thoroughly bewildered*]

Oh, look sir, look sir! Here's more of us. I prophesied this fellow couldn't drown while gallows stood on land! Now, Mr Blasphemy, who threw the grace of God overboard with his swearing, have you no oaths now you're on shore? Silent, are you, now you're on land? What's the news?

Bosun The best news is that we have found our king and our passengers; the next best, that our ship – which only three hours ago we said was split – is in one piece, shipshape and trimly rigged, as when we first put out to sea.

Ariel [*aside to* **Prospero**] Sir, I've done all this since I last left you.

Prospero [*aside to* **Ariel**] That's my clever spirit!

Alonso This is all quite uncanny. What's strange gets stranger. Tell me, how did you get here?

Boatswain If I did think, sir, I were well awake,
I'd strive to tell you. We were dead of sleep,
And – how we know not – all clapped under hatches;
Where, but even now, with strange and several noises
Of roaring, shrieking, howling, jingling chains,
And more diversity of sounds, all horrible,
We were awaked; straightway, at liberty;
Where we, in all our trim, freshly beheld
Our royal, good, and gallant ship; our master
Cap'ring to eye her: on a trice, so please you,
Even in a dream, were we divided from them,
And were brought moping hither.

Ariel [*Aside to* **Prospero**] Was't well done?

Prospero [*Aside to* **Ariel**] Bravely, my diligence. Thou shalt
be free.

Alonso This is as strange a maze as e'er men trod;
And there is in this business more than nature
Was ever conduct of: some oracle
Must rectify our knowledge.

Prospero Sir, my liege,
Do not infest your mind with beating on
The strangeness of this business; at picked leisure
Which shall be shortly single, I'll resolve you,
Which to you shall seem probable, of every
These happened accidents; till when, be cheerful,
And think of each thing well. [*Aside to* **Ariel**] Come hither,
spirit:
Set Caliban and his companions free;
Untie the spell. [*Exit* **Ariel**] How fares my gracious sir?
There are yet missing of your company
Some few odd lads that you remember not.

[*Enter* **Ariel,** *driving in* **Caliban, Stephano,** *and* **Trinculo,** *in their stolen apparel*]

Bosun If I thought I were wide awake, sir, I'd try to tell you. We were sound asleep and – how, we don't know – all imprisoned below decks. Then, just now, various weird noises of roaring, shrieking, howling, jangling of chains, and other varieties of sounds – all horrible! – awakened us. Immediately we were free. Unscathed, we saw our royal, good, and gallant ship again. The captain jumped for joy at the sight of her. In a jiffy, as it were in a dream, we were separated from the rest of the crew and brought, bewildered, here.

Ariel [*to* **Prospero**] Did I do it right?

Prospero [*to* **Ariel**] Splendidly, my speedy one. You shall be free.

Alonso This is as hard a puzzle as anyone ever set out to solve. And there's more to this than has a natural explanation. Some oracle must fill in the gaps in our knowledge.

Prospero My dear sir, don't bother your mind with the strangeness of this business. At our convenient leisure, soon and in private, I'll explain to your satisfaction all these things that have happened. Till then, be cheerful and regard everything as for the best. [*Aside to* **Ariel**] Come here, spirit. Set Caliban and his companions free. Untie the spell. [**Ariel** *goes. To* **Alonso**] Are you all right, my gracious sir? There are a few odd lads still missing from your company that you've forgotten.

[**Ariel** *returns, driving in* **Caliban, Stephano,** *and* **Trinculo,** *who are still wearing the stolen clothes*]

Stephano Every man shift for all the rest, and let no man take care for himself; for all is but fortune. Coragio, bully-monster, coragio!

Trinculo If these be true spies which I wear in my head, here's a goodly sight.

Caliban O Setebos, these be brave spirits indeed!
How fine my master is! I am afraid
He will chastise me.

Sebastian Ha, ha!
What things are these, my lord Antonio?
Will money buy 'em?

Antonio Very like; one of them
Is a plain fish, and, no doubt, marketable.

Prospero Mark but the badges of these men, my lords,
Then say if they be true. This mis-shapen knave,
His mother was a witch; and one so strong
That could control the moon, make flows and ebbs,
And deal in her command, without her power.
These three have robbed me; and this demi-devil –
For he's a bastard one – had plotted with them
To take my life. Two of these fellows you
Must know and own; this thing of darkness I
Acknowledge mine.

Caliban I shall be pinched to death.

Alonso Is not this Stephano, my drunken butler?

Sebastian He is drunk now: where had he wine?

Alonso And Trinculo is reeling ripe: where should they
Find this grand liquor that hath gilded 'em?
How cam'st thou in this pickle?

Trinculo I have been in such a pickle, since I saw you last,

Stephano [*drunk still, and getting his ideas muddled*] Every man for the rest, and don't look after yourself! It's all a matter of luck. Have courage!

Trinculo If my eyes aren't lying, this is a welcome sight!

Caliban [*admiring the assembled company*] Oh, the devil! These are splendid spirits indeed! How grand my master looks! I'm afraid he'll punish me.

Sebastian Ha, ha! Whatever are these, my lord Antonio? Will money buy them?

Antonio Probably. [*Eyeing* **Caliban**] One of them's certainly peculiar, with commercial value, no doubt!

Prospero Take a close look at what these men are wearing, my lords, then make up your minds about their honesty. [*Pointing to* **Caliban**] As for this misshapen knave, his mother was a witch, one so powerful that she could control the moon, make the oceans ebb and flow, and do the moon's work whenever she wished. These three have stolen from me, and this half-devil – he was misbegotten – plotted with them to take my life. Two of these fellows you must know and own. This devilish object [*pointing to* **Caliban**] is mine.

Caliban I'll be pinched to death!

Alonso Isn't this Stephano, my drunken butler?

Sebastian He's drunk now: where did he get the wine?

Alonso And Trinculo is tipsy. Where could they find this potent liquor that has sozzled them? [*To* **Trinculo**] How come you are so pickled?

Trinculo I've been in such a pickle since I last saw you that

that, I fear me, will never out of my bones: I shall not fear fly-blowing.

Sebastian Why, how now, Stephano!

Stephano O, touch me not; I am not Stephano, but a cramp.

Prospero You'd be King o' the isle, sirrah?

Stephano I should have been a sore one, then.

Alonso This is a strange thing as e'er I looked on. [*Pointing to* **Caliban**]

Prospero He is as disproportioned in his manners
As in his shape. Go, sirrah, to my cell;
Take with you your companions; as you look
To have my pardon, trim it handsomely.

Caliban Ay, that I will; and I'll be wise hereafter,
And seek for grace. What a thrice-double ass
Was I, to take this drunkard for a god,
And worship this dull fool!

Prospero Go to; away!

Alonso Hence, and bestow your luggage where you found it.

Sebastian Or stole it, rather.

[*Exeunt* **Caliban, Stephano** *and* **Trinculo**]

Prospero Sir, I invite your Highness and your train
To my poor cell, where you shall take your rest
For this one night; which, part of it, I'll waste
With such discourse as, I not doubt, shall make it
Go quick away: the story of my life,
And the particular accidents gone by
Since I came to this isle: and in the morn
I'll bring you to your ship, and so to Naples,

I'm preserved. There'll never be any flies on me.

Sebastian Greetings, Stephano! [*Slapping him on the back*]

Stephano [*wincing*] Oh, don't touch me! I'm not Stephano. I'm a walking cramp.

Prospero So you'd be king of the island, eh?

Stephano A sore one, if I had been.

Alonso [*pointing to* **Caliban**] I've never seen anything so peculiar.

Prospero He's as grotesque in his manners as he is in his shape. [*To* **Caliban**] Go to my cave, you. Take your companions with you. If you want my forgiveness, watch how you behave.

Caliban Yes, I certainly will. And I'll be sensible from now on and try to please. What an ass six times over I was to take this drunkard for a god and worship this jester!

Prospero All right. Off with you now!

Alonso Go, and put that stuff back where you found it.

Sebastian Or stole it more likely.

[**Stephano** *and* **Trinculo** *remove their finery and go, followed by* **Caliban**]

Prospero [*to* **Alonso**] Sir, I invite Your Highness and your followers to my poor cave, where you can rest for this one night. Part of it I'll spend in talk that will, I have no doubt, make time pass quickly. I'll tell you the story of my life, and the details of my residence on this island. In the morning, I'll take you to your ship; and then, to Naples, where I hope

Where I have hope to see the nuptial
Of these our dear-beloved solemnized;
And thence retire me to my Milan, where
Every third thought shall be my grave.

Alonso I long
To hear the story of your life, which must
Take the ear strangely.

Prospero I'll deliver all;
And promise you calm seas, auspicious gales,
And sail so expeditious, that shall catch
Your royal fleet far off. [*Aside to* **Ariel**] My Ariel, chick,
That is thy charge: then to the elements
Be free, and fare thou well! Please you, draw near.

[*Exeunt*]

Epilogue *spoken by* **Prospero**

Now my charms are all o'erthrown,
And what strength I have's mine own,
Which is most faint: now, 'tis true,
I must be here confined by you,
Or sent to Naples. Let me not,
Since I have my dukedom got,
And pardoned the deceiver, dwell
In this bare island by your spell;
But release me from my bands
With the help of your good hands:
Gentle breath of yours my sails
Must fill, or else my project fails,
Which was to please. Now I want
Spirits to enforce, Art to enchant;
And my ending is despair,
Unless I be relieved by prayer,

to see the marriage of our loved ones solemnized. Afterwards, I'll retire to Milan, where I shall be much preoccupied with thoughts of death.

Alonso I long to hear the story of your life, which must be a most remarkable one.

Prospero I'll tell you everything, and I promise you calm seas, favorable winds, and a voyage so speedy that you'll catch up with your royal fleet, distant though it is. [*Aside to* **Ariel**] My Ariel, chick: those are your orders. Then be free as air, and fare you well! [*To the company, indicating his cave*] Will you join me?

[*They all go in*]

Epilogue [*spoken by the actor who plays* **Prospero**]

My magic power's now overthrown,
What remains is me alone:
A feeble man. Now, it's true,
I must be here detained by you
Or sent to Naples. Let me not –
Since I have my dukedom got
And pardoned the deceiver – dwell
On this bare island by your spell.
But release me from my bands
With the help of your good hands.
To speed me forth, your praise I need
If my objective's to succeed –
Which was to please. Now I want
Spirits to compel, Art to enchant;
I shall end in sad despair
Unless I'm aided by a prayer

Which pierces so, that it assaults
Mercy itself, and frees all faults.
As you from crimes would pardoned be,
Let your indulgence set me free.

[*Exit*]

So potent Mercy can't refuse
Her pity; and my faults excuse.
As you from crimes would pardoned be,
Let your applause now set me free.

[*He leaves the stage*]

Activities

Characters

Search the text (in either the original or the modern version) to find answers to the following questions. They will help you to form personal opinions about the major characters in the play. *Record any relevant quotations in Shakespeare's own words.*

Prospero

1 **a** How do we know from Miranda's first words to Prospero in *Act I Scene 2* that he is a magician?

b How do we know from his reply that he is a benevolent one?

c What is the outward symbol of his magical skills?

d What magic does he practice on Miranda in this scene?

2 In *Act I Scene 2*, Prospero explains how he came to be on the island with his daughter.

a What does he tell us of his former rank and reputation?

b What do we learn of the importance to him of his studies?

c How do we know that he was a man who trusted others?

d What evidence is there that he continued to trust others when he settled on the island?

3 Prospero's "project" is achieved with the help of the spirit Ariel. From the evidence in *Act I Scene 2*,

a how did Prospero come to be Ariel's master?

b what promises did Prospero make about Ariel's length of service?

c what do we learn of Prospero's character from his response to Ariel's complaints?

4 Prospero's other servant is the monster Caliban.

a How did Prospero treat Caliban when he first arrived on the island?

b What happened to change Prospero's attitude?

c Choose some words and phrases of Prospero's from *Act I Scene 2* that are typical of his relationship with Caliban throughout the play.

5 Part of Prospero's "project" is to bring Miranda and Ferdinand together.

a What evidence is there in *Act I Scene 2* that Prospero hopes they will fall in love?

b Why does Prospero treat Ferdinand "so ungently"?

c How does he use his magical powers to further his plans?

d Is Prospero's anger at this point genuine or feigned?

6 In *Act III Scene 1*, Ferdinand says of Prospero: "he's composed of harshness."

a Illustrate from Prospero's own words in this scene the tender side of his nature.

b Find three episodes in the play where he exercises severity.

7 **a** In *Act III Scene 3*, which words of Prospero's indicate that his "project" has succeeded as far as the nobles are concerned?

b Which words of Gonzalo's confirm the success?

8 **a** At the beginning of *Act IV Scene 1*, how does Prospero show that as a father he is

i loving
ii proud
iii caring?

b How does he show that as a host he is

i considerate
ii polite?

9 At the end of *Act IV Scene 1*, Prospero begins to deal with the conspiracy against his own life.

a How do we know from what Miranda says that Prospero is angry?

b How do we know from what Prospero says that the anger is deeply felt?

c What action has Ariel taken on Prospero's behalf to punish the conspirators?

d What action does Prospero personally take in this scene?

10 *In Act V Scene 1*, Prospero's "project" reaches completion.

a At the beginning of this long scene, what three important factors are working in Prospero's favor against those who did him "high wrongs"?

b What reasons does Prospero give for treating his enemies mercifully?

c Do you think Ariel's comments influence him?

11 Having decided that "the rarer action is/In virtue than in vengeance," Prospero addresses the royal party as its members stand "spell-stopped" inside the magic circle.

a How does he deal with each of the four principals in turn?

b How does each react?

c With which two members of the party does Prospero most closely relate, and why?

d Which of the four says least?

12 Two things remain for Prospero to do before giving Ariel his freedom.

a What is the first?

b What is the second?

Are both consistent with Prospero's policy of kindness toward everyone?

Miranda

1 From her first appearance in *Act I Scene 2*, Miranda shows herself to be

- **a** tenderhearted
- **b** compliant
- **c** attentive
- **d** polite
- **e** sympathetic
- **f** self-effacing
- **g** appreciative

Find evidence from the text to demonstrate these qualities.

2 In the dialogue with Caliban in *Act I Scene 2*, Miranda's speech beginning "Abhorred slave" (line 355) is sometimes attributed to Prospero. Read it carefully, then

- **a** explain why there might be doubt about the speaker, and
- **b** decide which you would choose if you were editing the text or producing the play on stage.

3 Ferdinand is drawn to Prospero's cell (cave) by Ariel's playing and singing.

- **a** At first, Miranda thinks he is a spirit. Why should this be?
- **b** Next, she learns he is mortal. Explain how she can rightly say "This/Is the third man that e'er I saw."
- **c** In her behavior toward Ferdinand, she confirms Prospero's belief that "At the first sight/They have changed eyes." Which of her words show that she has, indeed fallen in love?

4 Ferdinand and Miranda are seemingly alone together at the beginning of *Act III Scene 1*.

- **a** Why "seemingly"?
- **b** How does Miranda demonstrate her tenderheartedness
  - i in words
  - ii in deeds?

- **c** How does she show that love for Ferdinand rivals duty to her father?
- **d** How does she show that she is always mindful of Prospero's teachings?

5 As early as *Act IV Scene 1*, Miranda's "vexations" are at an end and Prospero has given his "rich gift" to Ferdinand.

- **a** What condition is placed upon the couple?
- **b** How does Prospero's entertainment, performed by Ariel and the spirits, relate to the lovers?

6 In *Act V Scene 1*

- **a** How is Miranda's sweet nature demonstrated by her attitude to the game of chess?
- **b** How is it further shown by her reactions on seeing the royal party?
- **c** How are her last words in the play consistent with her father's attitude to human beings?
- **d** Is there any reason to question Ferdinand's description of her in *Act III Scene 1* as "so perfect, and so peerless"?

Ferdinand

1 The first reference to Ferdinand is in *Act I Scene 2* in Ariel's description of the storm-tossed ship.

- **a** What was noteworthy about Ferdinand's behavior during the tempest?
- **b** What do we learn from Francisco in *Act II Scene 1* of Ferdinand's behavior in the water?
- **c** According to Ariel, how did Ferdinand respond to being (as he thought) a sole survivor?

2 Ariel leads Ferdinand to Prospero's cell, where he meets Miranda.

a How do his first words to her show him to be
   i respectful
   ii modest
   iii deeply in love?

b How do we know from what Miranda says that he is handsome?

c How does his behavior when threatened show that he is brave?

3 In *Act III Scene 1*, Ferdinand is given a menial task by Prospero in order to test him.

a Ferdinand says he is a "patient log-man" for Miranda's sake. Find the words which Prospero overhears confirming the sincerity of his love.

b How do we know that Ferdinand has been attracted to women before?

c Why does Ferdinand consider Miranda to be in a class of her own?

d How do we know from the manner of his proposal that Ferdinand is as modest and unassuming as Miranda?

e How do we know from *Act IV Scene 1* that he is equally virtuous?

4 Ferdinand's final words show that he has a major part to play in the process of reconciliation.

a Explain how Ferdinand brings Alonso and Prospero into a closer relationship.

b Explain why Gonzalo rejoices at the marriage between Ferdinand and Miranda.

5 Prospero describes the tender love scene between Ferdinand and Miranda (*Act III Scene 1*) as a "fair encounter/Of two most rare affections!" In what ways is Ferdinand similar to Miranda?

Ariel

1 How do Ariel's first words in *Act I Scene 2*

a sum up his purpose in the play?

b illustrate his relationship to Prospero?

2 In the same scene, what do we learn of

a his past history?

b the range of his powers?

c the quality of his service to Prospero?

d his one ambition?

3 In *Act I Scene 2*, Ariel is both praised and rebuked.

a What can be inferred about Ariel's character from the way in which he reacts to Prospero's censure?

b How often, and in what tender terms, does Prospero show his affection for Ariel in this scene?

c Which of the two attitudes do you regard as the more genuine in Prospero?

4 Also in *Act I Scene 2*, Ariel uses his powers of invisibility and music to carry out Prospero's orders.

a i How do we know from what Ferdinand says that Ariel's music subdued the storm?

ii Which words in the song refer to this calming influence?

b i How do we know that Ferdinand found the music irresistible?

ii Which of his words refer to its calming influence?

c How does Ariel use song in

i *Act II Scene 1*

ii *Act V Scene 1*?

5 **a** In *Act III Scene 2*, Ariel uses his powers of invisibility again.

i Explain how this befits the comic purposes of the scene.

ii Explain how it also helps to create discord between the three conspirators.

b He also uses music: a tabor and a pipe.

i Which of the conspirators is not afraid to hear it, and why?

ii Which says he is not afraid, but possibly might be?

iii Which is certainly afraid?

c Some editors think Caliban suggests following the music, as in this edition. Others think the line belongs to Trinculo. Which do you think is right and why?

6 **a** Ariel intervenes in *Act III Scene 3* to sweep away the banquet that has been laid before the king and his party.

i What is his disguise?

ii Which three men does he denounce?

iii What does he say is his purpose in addressing them?

iv What does he say is to be Alonso's punishment?

v How can Alonso avoid it?

b Prospero makes two comments on Ariel's performance, one in this scene, and the other in *Act IV Scene 1*. What is his opinion of it?

7 In *Act IV Scene 1*, Ariel is commissioned to perform "such another trick."

a How do we know that he will obey Prospero speedily?

b How do we know that he is touchingly dependent on Prospero's affection?

c How do we know from his remarks after the masque ends that he is afraid of Prospero's quick temper?

d How do we know from the hunting episode at the end of the scene that he can scourge others enthusiastically?

8 Ariel earns his freedom in *Act V Scene 1*.

a At what time does he expect to be released?

b What tasks does he perform

i in connection with the royal party

  ii in connection with the mariners
  iii in connection with the three conspirators
  iv for Prospero personally?

- **c** Which lines in this scene
  - i emphasize that Ariel is not a mortal
  - ii prompt Prospero to announce "the sole drift" of his purpose in bringing his enemies to the island?
- **d** Why do you think Shakespeare made the release of Ariel to be Prospero's last act in the play?

Caliban

1 Caliban's first appearance is in *Act I Scene 2*.

- **a** Explain the connection between Ariel's past history and Caliban's.
- **b** From the information in this scene and that given in *Act II Scene 2*, deduce the kind of life Caliban led when the island was his.
- **c** How, at first, did Prospero treat Caliban?
- **d** How, at first, did Caliban treat Prospero?
- **e** What did Miranda teach Caliban that she and her father had reason to regret later?
- **f** What was Caliban's offense?
- **g** From the information in this scene and *Act II Scene 2*, what kind of life did Caliban lead after his fall from grace?
- **h** What punishments has he suffered and does he fear, according to what we learn from this scene and *Act II Scene 2*?

2 Caliban encounters Trinculo and Stephano in *Act II Scene 2*.

- **a** What are the reasons Caliban thinks the two cast-aways are divine in origin?
- **b** How does this provide a source of comedy?

- **c** How does Stephano respond to Caliban's homage?
- **d** What is Trinculo's attitude to the "moon-calf"?

3 In *Act III Scene 2* Caliban proposes the murder of Prospero.

- **a** How is the brutality of Caliban counterbalanced by comedy involving
  - i knockabout farce
  - ii mistaken identity
  - iii naive self-abasement
  - iv absurd vanity
  - v the supernatural?
- **b** What side of Caliban's nature is revealed in his speech describing his delight in the "sounds and sweet airs" of the island?

4 From evidence in *Act IV Scene 1*,

- **a** how do we know that Prospero takes the plot against his life very seriously?
- **b** how do we know from Prospero's remarks that he believes Caliban is incurably savage?
- **c** how is it made clear that Caliban is more astute than his fellow-conspirators?
- **d** in what two ways are the trio physically punished in this scene?

5 Caliban last appears in *Act V Scene 1*.

- **a** In what way is his reaction to the sight of the royal party similar to that of Miranda earlier in the scene?
- **b** What does he say that indicates repentance?
- **c** What hint is there that Prospero is willing to forgive?
- **d** Does the prospect of a reformation explain why Caliban's speech is predominantly in blank verse?

Alonso

1 From the evidence provided by Prospero in *Act I Scene 2*, explain why Alonso is "a man of sin."

2 In *Act II Scene 1*,

  a what two reasons does Alonso give for his personal sorrow?

  b what reason does Sebastian give for saying to his brother "the fault's your own"?

3 In *Act III Scene 3*, Ariel denounces Prospero's three enemies, naming Alonso in particular.

  a What does Ariel say is to be Alonso's punishment?

  b How can it be mitigated?

  c According to Prospero and Gonzalo, how does Alonso react to Ariel's pronouncements?

  d How do we know from Alonso's last speech in this scene that he admits his guilt?

  e What is the effect on his mind?

4 We learn at the beginning of *Act V Scene 1* of Prospero's purpose in planning and executing his "project."

  a What comment of Ariel's on Alonso's predicament prompts Prospero to reveal "the sole drift" of his "purpose"?

  b What is Alonso's immediate response after regaining his sanity?

5 a How, at first, does Alonso believe he shares a grief with Prospero?

  b How, in the end, does he share a joy with him?

Sebastian and Antonio

1 The steps leading to Antonio's betrayal of his brother are outlined by Prospero in *Act I Scene 2*. Trace them.

2 Antonio and Sebastian are birds of a feather.

a Show how *Act II Scene 1* confirms this.

b Give examples of their (i) disrespect; (ii) scorn; (iii) indelicacy; (iv) sarcasm.

c How does Sebastian express insensitivity toward his brother's feelings?

3 Antonio initiates the assassination plot.

a He puts a series of leading questions to Sebastian. Identify them.

b He also puts forward a number of persuasive arguments. What are they?

c What is Antonio's answer to Sebastian's reference to conscience?

d What finally convinces Sebastian that he should act?

e What is to be Antonio's reward for the murder of Alonso and Gonzalo?

4 The villainy of Antonio and Sebastian is shown again in *Act III Scene 3*.

a What is Antonio's comment when Alonso concedes that Ferdinand is dead?

b How do we know that Antonio and Sebastian are as determined as ever to proceed with their plans?

c What is Prospero's comment on them?

d What is Ariel's?

e How is their reaction to guilt different from that of Alonso's?

5 In *Act V Scene 1*, Antonio and Sebastian enter spellbound and distracted.

a Speaking as an observer, Prospero identifies their crimes before restoring them to sanity. What does he say is going on in their minds while "ignorant fumes . . . mantle/Their clearer reason"?

b Prospero tells "the brace of lords" that "at this time" he will "tell no tales." Do you think this means
   i he does not wish to spoil the atmosphere of reconciliation and forgiveness by revealing the assassination plot, or
   ii that he may do so later?

6 **a** The behavior of Antonio and Sebastian after Prospero's revelation indicates shock.
   i How does Sebastian show this?
   ii How does Antonio?

b The interludes with the bosun and "the few odd lads" (Caliban, Stephano, and Trinculo) give them time to recover.
   i What evidence is there that they are unchanged by their experiences?
   ii Which of the two seems to be the most confident as the play ends?

Gonzalo

1 In the list of characters provided in the 1623 Folio, Gonzalo is described as "an honest old Counsellor."

a Show how Prospero's references to him in *Act I Scene 2* confirm this.

b What other flattering words are spoken of him by Prospero in *Act III Scene 3* and *Act V Scene 1*?

c What is there about him that would have touched Ariel, had he been human?

2 Antonio and Sebastian are scornful of him. Illustrate their contempt for "this Sir Prudence" from episodes in *Act II Scene 1*:

a before Gonzalo falls asleep, and

b during the planning of the assassination.

3 Gonzalo is "a loyal sir."

- **a** How did he serve Alonso at the time of Prospero's banishment?
- **b** How does he continue to show loyalty to the king on board ship in *Act I Scene 1*?
- **c** What examples can you find in *Act II Scene 1* of
  - i his attempts to comfort the king
  - ii his attempts to amuse the king
  - iii his attempts to protect the king?
- **d** What orders does he give at the end of *Act III Scene 3* that
  - i indicate his awareness of the long-standing injustice done to Prospero, and
  - ii show his compassionate nature?

4 Gonzalo is undoubtedly garrulous.

- **a** How many times does Alonso ask him to be quiet in *Act II Scene 1*?
- **b** How do Antonio and Sebastian mock him for
  - i speaking too often
  - ii speaking pedantically
  - iii speaking with feeble wit
  - iv speaking inconsistently?

5 In the final scene of the play, Gonzalo has

- **a** the task of summing up. How do his words emphasize the happy ending to the play?
- **b** the pleasure of being proved right. How do his last words to the bosun link the end of the play to its beginning and add to the good-humored atmosphere?

Stephano and **Trinculo**

1 The drunken butler and the court jester provide the comic subplot in *The Tempest*.

- **a** Mistaken identity is the source of humor in *Act II Scene 2*.

- i For what does Trinculo mistake Caliban?
- ii For what does Caliban mistake Trinculo?
- iii For what does Stephano mistake Trinculo and Caliban together?

b After the three are properly identified,

- i Stephano emerges as the natural leader. Why?
- ii Trinculo takes second place and derides Caliban. Why does the scorn of a jester highlight the comic relationship?
- iii the bottle assumes a special significance. What is it?

2 In *Act III Scene 2*, Stephano and Trinculo set up court.

a How do we know from Stephano's first words that he is

- i irresponsible as a leader
- ii vain?

b How do Trinculo's first words astutely sum up the instability of their government?

c What references are there in the scene to normal court procedures?

d How do the foolish ambitions of Stephano and Trinculo echo the real ones of Alonso, Sebastian, and Antonio?

e How does the intervention of Ariel ensure that the wickedness of their plot is subsidiary to the comedy of their relationship?

3 The "foul conspiracy" which so disturbs Prospero in *Act IV Scene 1* is frustrated

a by Ariel. How does he use his magical powers to cool the "varlets" who are "red-hot with drinking"?

b by Prospero. What is his trick?

c How is the foolishness of Stephano and Trinculo contrasted with the wisdom of their subject, Caliban, in this episode?

d Why is the robust physical punishment amusing in the context of this scene?

4 Stephano, Trinculo and Caliban, still wearing their stolen garments, are the last to be dealt with publicly before the play ends.

a Prospero introduces them as "a few odd lads." What does this suggest about his attitude to them?

b How do we know that Stephano and Trinculo are drunk?

c Which words of Caliban's sum up the subplot?

d How does the verbal scourging of the malefactors help to bring

i a spirit of unity and

ii an element of comedy to the concluding moments of the play?

Structure, plot, and themes

1 *The Tempest* is, structurally, the simplest of Shakespeare's plays.

- **a** The time scheme is clearly indicated. From the evidence in *Act I Scene 2,*
  - i at what hour in the afternoon does Prospero begin his "project"
  - ii by what hour is it to be completed?
- **b** The action is confined to the island and "nigh shore."
  - i Into how many scenes is the play divided?
  - ii How many locations are indicated?

2 The play has three centers of dramatic interest:
The progress of the royal party
The progress of the Ferdinand/Miranda relationship
The progress of the Caliban/Stephano/Trinculo conspiracy.

- **a** Overall, the objective is the restoration of Prospero's duke-dom after his long period of hardship and suffering. Show how hardship and suffering are essential factors in the play's three strands.
- **b**
  - i As an agent of Prospero, Ariel plays a part in each strand. Show how.
  - ii To what extent does Ariel's own story help to bind the strands together?

3 Magic enables Prospero to manipulate the inhabitants of the island.

- **a** How are the mariners and their ship affected by magic? (*Act I Scene 2, Act V Scene 1*)
- **b** Which characters are magically put to sleep? (*Act I Scene 2, Act II Scene 1*)
- **c** Music and dance are used in magical contexts. (*Act I Scene*

2, *Act II Scene 1, Act III Scene 2, Act III Scene 3,* and *Act V Scene 1*) What is the effect in each case?

d Why is invisibility important in *Act I Scene 2, Act II Scene 1, Act III Scene 2, Act III Scene 3,* and *Act IV Scene 1*?

e How are the magic spells cast in *Act I Scene 2* and *Act V Scene 1* important to the development of the plot?

f What is the role of the Spirits who appear in various guises in *Act III Scene 3* and *Act IV Scene 1*?

g In what forms does Ariel present himself in *Act 1 Scene 2, Act III Scene 3,* and *Act IV Scene 1*?

4 Spectacle is a feature of *Act III Scene 3* (the dumb show) and *Act IV Scene 1* (the masque).

a Each is generously praised. By whom?

b Each comes to an end with the aid of a sound effect: "thunder and lightning" in the first case; "a strange, hollow, and confused noise" in the second. Explain why each is appropriate to the dramatic context.

5 The play ends in a spirit of reconciliation.

a At the end of *Act IV Scene 1,* Prospero has all his enemies at his mercy. What does he say in *Act V Scene 1* to explain why he does not exact vengeance?

b Is the penitence of those who have done wrong

i convincing, or

ii merely assumed?

Close reading

Read the original Shakespeare and (if necessary) the modern transcription to gain an understanding of the speeches and extracts below. Then concentrate entirely on the original in answering the questions.

1 *"To every article./I boarded the king's ship; . . ." (Act I Scene 2, lines 195–196)*

- **a** What is the question answered by the brief first sentence?
- **b** Ariel "flamed amazement." How does he convey a sense of speed in the opening lines?
- **c** Which verbs make his description vivid?
- **d** Why are adjectives effective in the latter part of the speech and unnecessary at the beginning of it?
- **e** Sight, sound, and smell are featured in this account of the tempest. Identify examples of each.
- **f** How does Ariel establish scale in his narrative?

2 *"I must eat my dinner./This island's mine, by Sycorax my mother, . . . " (Act 1 Scene 2, lines 335–36)*

- **a** Caliban and Prospero have just exchanged harsh words. Why does the simple opening sentence create a measure of sympathy for the monster?
- **b** There are three suggestions in the speech that Caliban has a limited vocabulary. Identify them and say how they add to the pathos of his situation.
- **c** How is tenderness contrasted with hatred?
- **d** How is the evil of Sycorax vividly conveyed?
- **e** How does Caliban suggest he is the victim of harsh injustice?
- **f** What hint is there here of the pride of the noble savage?

3 *"I' th' commonwealth I would by contraries . . ."* (*Act II Scene 1, line 145*)

a Gonzalo's description of his Utopia has been traced to an essay by the French author Montaigne, who defended "natural" men against their "civilized" counterparts. Some critics think Shakespeare was mocking Montaigne's viewpoint because Gonzalo is the spokesman. Others think that the jeers of Sebastian and Antonio imply that Shakespeare sympathized with it. What is your opinion?

b List the features of civilization which Gonzalo would abolish, and suggest reasons why an ideal state would be better without them.

c Why would the violent aspects of "civilized" society disappear?

d Does Gonzalo have a place for work in his commonwealth?

e What inconsistency is mocked by Sebastian and Antonio?

f What else do they sneer at?

4 *"Be not afeard; the isle is full of noises, . . ."* (*Act III Scene 2, line 129*)

Elsewhere, Caliban shows that he has a profound knowledge of the island and its physical resources, good and bad.

a Here, he responds sensitively to
  i its music. Which words convey his appreciation of melody and orchestration?
  ii vocal sounds. How might voices be used to make him sleep so deeply?

b What is poignant about his recollection of dreams?

c Caliban's tenses change during this speech. Identify where this happens, and say whether you agree that the effect is to convey Caliban's state of imaginative enchantment.

5 *"You are three men of sin, whom Destiny . . ." (Act III Scene 3, line 57)*

- **a** Why would Ariel's "men of sin" be shocked even before he begins to speak?
- **b** Ariel accuses them in words that are predominantly of one syllable. Which phrases are thereby emphasized?
- **c** The stage direction "*Alonso, Sebastian, etc., draw their swords*" comes at the end of a sentence. Why might it be better placed after "I have made you mad"?
- **d** There is no stage direction suggesting the royal party cannot wield their swords. Where might one be aptly placed?
- **e** What suggestions are there in the passage that nature itself has taken revenge for unnatural deeds?
- **f** Two words convey Alonso's sentence: how does their sound echo their sense?
- **g** "Whose wraths to guard you from" can either refer to "seas and shores" or "the powers." Which do you think makes best sense?

6 *"You do look, my son, in a moved sort, . . ." (Act IV Scene 1, line 146)*

- **a** Critics have been puzzled by Prospero's reference to Ferdinand's distress: they point out that it is Prospero who is "in some passion," not his future son-in-law. What might be the explanation?
- **b** There are two similes in the passage. ("like the baseless fabric of this vision" and "like this insubstantial pageant faded"). They are very similar. Where else in this speech does Prospero repeat himself for emphatic purposes?
- **c** Which two lines stand out in contrast with the rest because they refer to things of substance?
- **d** In several of Shakespeare's plays, "rounded" means "crowned." What difference could this make to the conventional interpretation of this famous line?

e What is the force of the adjective in the phrase "our little life"?

f Comment on Prospero's admission in the last lines of this speech.

7 *"I told you, sir, they were red-hot with drinking; . . ."* (*Act IV Scene 1, line 173*)

a Why is this episode described by Ariel and not acted out on stage?

b Ariel begins by saying "I told you, sir."
  i Do you think this proves that a scene from the play has been lost or cut out (as some scholars think) or
  ii do you regard it as an example of the dramatist's skill in inventing natural dialogue, which is what others believe?

c Which words suggest that Prospero was in real danger from the drunkards?

d Two similes in the passage both illustrate and demean: trace them, and explain their dual effectiveness.

e How does Ariel convey the discomfiture of the conspirators by the use of contrasting adjectives?

f Explain why Ariel's final statement has a coarse humor.

8 *"Ye elves of hills, brooks, standing lakes, and groves, . . ."* (*Act V Scene 1, lines 33–57*)

a Prospero addresses four "weak masters": list them, and say what we learn of the activities of three of them.

b i List the ways in which Prospero has used his "potent Art."
  ii Which of the feats he mentions seems impossible considering the nature of the island?

c Prospero's final act as a magician is to "require some heavenly music." Cite some other references to the hypnotic effect of music in the play.

d In abjuring his magical powers, Prospero details the three stages that are necessary. Explain them.

9 *"A solemn air, and the best comforter . . ." (Act V Scene 1, line 58)*

a In Elizabethan slang, "boiled" meant "betrayed" so there are two possible interpretations of Prospero's reference to Alonso's madness. Which do you prefer, and why?

b How do we know that Gonzalo is tearful here?

c How does Prospero's use of (i) simile and (ii) metaphor help to describe the slow process of recovery from his "charm"?

d Consider the adjectives used to describe Gonzalo, and compare them with Antonio's derisory remarks about him in *Act II Scene 1*. Is there a case for thinking that Prospero's emotions have got the better of him?

e The "three men of sin" are addressed separately.

i Is their guilt equal?

ii On the evidence of their subsequent behavior, is their remorse equal?

f Prospero sends Ariel for two articles related to his princely status. What does Caliban say of him later that suggests Ariel returns with an ampler wardrobe?

10 *Epilogue*

Experts have interpreted these twenty lines in several ways.

a Some believe Shakespeare is saying farewell to his audience and seeking consent to retire to Stratford.

b Others believe it is a conventional appeal for applause by an actor who steps out of his part.

Explain how both interpretations are possible, and say which you favor.

Examination questions

The following are typical of the kind of questions found on exams.

1. "A savage and deformed slave." How far do you agree with this description of Caliban?
2. Illustrate from his speeches and actions throughout *The Tempest* the character of Prospero and his use of magical powers.
3. "Caliban is a more original and a more important creation than Ariel." Describe both characters and their role in the action of the play, and say whether you agree or disagree with this statement.
4. "Prospero is a man with the power of a god." What are the advantages and disadvantages for the dramatist in creating such a character?
5. What part does the supernatural play in the action of *The Tempest*?
6. In what ways is music used to enhance the appeal of *The Tempest*, and to what extent is it important to the plot?
7. Explain and illustrate the dramatic significance of (a) the dumb show in *Act III Scene 3* and (b) the masque in *Act IV Scene 1*.
8. Choose two scenes in which Stephano and Trinculo appear, and illustrate the comic element which they provide.
9. There are two murderous plots in *The Tempest*. Describe the purpose of each and say how they are prevented.
10. Describe the part played by Gonzalo (a) in Prospero's banishment and (b) as a survivor of the shipwreck.
11. How does the love affair between Ferdinand and Miranda illustrate that "the course of true love never did run smooth"?

12 Describe the part played by Sebastian and Antonio in *The Tempest* after they are shipwrecked, and say whether Prospero's treatment of them is dramatically convincing in the context of the play.

13 What do we learn of Prospero's character from his treatment of (a) Caliban and (b) Ariel?

14 To what extent do you consider that *The Tempest* depends for its success on spectacle rather than on the resolution of a dramatic conflict?

15 What case is there, if any, for sympathizing with Caliban?

16 Critics have described the central theme of *The Tempest* as "repentance and forgiveness." Show by reference to Prospero's actions and statements the extent to which this theme gives the play its enduring interest.

17 "Each of the characters in the subplot – Stephano, Trinculo and Caliban – in some way or other can be shown to have a counterpart in the main plot." Choose any two characters and illustrate the truth or otherwise of this remark.

18 What could be the reasons for regarding *The Tempest* as a play "better seen than read"?

19 How successful is Shakespeare in the first scene of the play in (a) depicting a storm at sea and (b) differentiating between his characters?

20 Prospero has been described as "humorless, self-centered and abrupt." Account for his appeal to (a) actors and (b) audiences.

One-word-answer quiz

1 How old was Miranda when she left Milan?

2 How many years had Prospero and Miranda spent on the island?

3 Who was the first man to abandon the king of Naples' ship?

4 Who was the third man ever to be seen by Miranda?

5 What game are Ferdinand and Miranda playing when Prospero reveals them to his guests?

6 What had quit (abandoned) the "rotten carcase of a butt" in which Prospero and Miranda sailed to the island?

7 Who was in charge of the operation, ordered by Alonso, that resulted in Prospero's expulsion?

8 On what sea did the king's fleet reassemble after the storm?

9 Why was Sycorax marooned on the island, not executed, for her crimes?

10 Whose complexion was "perfect gallows"?

11 By how long did Prospero say he would shorten Ariel's period of service if he behaved?

12 In what kind of tree did Prospero threaten to imprison Ariel if he complained?

13 For how long would he keep him there?

14 After Ariel has been reprimanded for ingratitude, what shape does he take at Prospero's request?

15 Into what kind of tree was Ariel confined by Sycorax?

16 For how many years was he imprisoned?

17 What musical instrument did Ariel use to lead the drunkards into the "filthy mantled pool"?

18 What nocturnal sport does Sebastian say he would pursue if the moon went five weeks without changing?

19 How many inches of steel did Antonio say would put Alonso "to bed forever"?

20 Where did Ariel put the sailors after the storm?

21 Where did Ariel hide the king's ship after the storm?

22 Where was Sycorax born?

23 What was the name of the god she served?

24 Who is referred to as "Sir Prudence"?

25 How many speakers are there in the masque performed to entertain Ferdinand and Miranda?

26 What was the name of King Alonso's daughter?

27 Whom did she marry?

28 Whose snores, according to Sebastian, had meaning?

29 Which creatures does Caliban say "mow and chatter at me,/ And after bite me"?

30 Who cried "Hell is empty,/And all the devils are here" as he abandoned ship?

31 How many furlongs of sea was Gonzalo prepared to give for an acre of barren ground?

32 How many leagues did Stephano claim he swam to reach shore after the shipwreck?

33 Who "suffered with those that I saw suffer"?

34 Who, according to Antonio, is "this ancient morsel"?

35 What does Caliban say is the one advantage of having learned to speak?

36 What does Prospero accuse Ferdinand of being, when they first meet?

37 Antonio makes a bet with Sebastian about who shall speak first after a silence. What was the stake?

38 Who *did* speak first?

39 Who won the bet?

40 According to Trinculo, how many doits would "holiday fools" pay to see a dead Indian?

41 What was it that "hereditary sloth" taught Sebastian to do?

42 Which character describes in detail a Utopian system for governing the island?

43 Which character accuses Alonso of being responsible for the death of his own son?

44 At approximately what time of day do we first meet Ariel?

45 By what time of day is all Prospero's business concluded?

46 What was Sycorax's shape in her old age?

47 Who said that Tunis and Carthage were the same place?

48 Who, according to Antonio, was "a delicate wench"?

49 How many "leagues beyond man's life" did the queen of Tunis live?

50 On which continent were the garments of the shipwrecked nobles first worn?

What's missing?

Complete the following quotations:

1 You taught me language; and my profit on't/Is, . . .

2 Misery acquaints a man with . . .

3 What! I say, My foot my . . . ?

4 We are such stuff as dreams are made on . . .

5 All things in common Nature should produce/Without sweat or endeavour: . . .

6 You fools! I and my fellows/Are ministers of Fate . . .

7 Oh, out of that "no hope"/What great hope have you! No hope that way is . . .

8 When we were boys,/Who would believe that there were mcuntaineers . . .

9 O, I have suffered/With . . .

10 For all the rest,/They'll take suggestion as . . .

11 Oh, she is/Ten times more gentle than her father's crabbed . . .

12 I'll break my staff,/Bury it certain fathoms in the earth . . .

13 They are both in either's powers; but this swift business I must uneasy make lest . . .

14 Where the bee sucks, there suck I . . .

15 Thou dost snore distinctly; . . .

16 They say there's but five upon this isle; we are three of them; if . . .

17 His forward voice, now, is to speak well of his friend; his backward voice . . .

18 I have great comfort from this fellow; . . . . his complexion is perfect gallows.

19 All three of them are desperate: their great guilt . . .

20 Look, he's winding up the watch of his wit; by and by . . .

21 I,/Beyond all limit of what else i' th' world,/Do . . .

22 The truth you speak doth lack some gentleness,/And time to speak it in: you . . .

23 She that is Queen of Tunis; she . . .

24 I might call him/A thing divine; for nothing natural . . .

25 But you, my brace of lords, were I so minded, I here could . . .

26 Before you can say "come" and "go"/And breathe twice, and cry "so, so" . . .

27 What a thrice-double ass/Was I . . .

28 I should sin/To think but nobly of my grandmother: . . .

29 If thou neglect'st, or dost unwillingly/What I command, I'll . . .

30 The dropsy drown this fool! What do you mean . . . ?

31 Remember,/First to possess his books; for without them . . .

32 Oh, brave new world,/That . . .

33 These our actors,/As I foretold you, were all spirits, and . . .

34 Methinks our garments are now as fresh as . . .

35 If these be true spies which I wear in my head . . .

36 You are three men of sin, whom Destiny . . .

37 'Ban, 'Ban, Cacaliban . . .

38 Look thou be true; do not give dalliance/Too much the rein . . .

39 Earth's increase, foison plenty,/Barns and garners never empty . . .

40 If thou more murmur'st, I will rend an oak,/And . . .

41 No more yet of this;/For 'tis a chronicle of day by day,/Not . . .

42 You sunburn'd sicklemen, of August weary,/Come hither . . .

43 There be that can rule Naples/As well as . . .

44 And set it down/With gold on lasting pillars: in one voyage . . .

45 Be not afeard; the isle is full of noises, . . .

46 There's nothing ill can dwell in such a temple:/If the ill spirit . . .

47 Now my charms are all o'erthrown, . . .

48 You are gentlemen of brave mettle: you would . . .

49 Yes, for a score of kingdoms you should wrangle,/And I would call it . . .

50 All the infections that the sun sucks up/From bogs, fens, flats, . . .

At last! Shakespeare in Language everyone can understand...

SHAKESPEARE MADE EASY Series

Scene 7

Macbeth's castle. Enter a **sewer** *directing divers servants. Then enter* **Macbeth**.

Macbeth If it were done, when 'tis done, then 'twere well
It were done quickly: if th' assassination
Could trammel up the consequence, and catch,
With his surcease, success; that but this blow
Might be the be-all and the end-all here,
But here, upon this bank and shoal of time,
We'd jump the life to come. But in these cases
We still have judgement here: that we but teach
Blood instructions, which being taught return
To plague th'inventor: this even-handed justice
Commends th'ingredience of our poisoned chalice
To our own lips. He's here in double trust:
First, as I am his kinsman and his subject,
Strong both against the deed: then, as his host,
Who should against his murderer shut the door,
Not bear the knife myself. Besides, this Duncan
Hath borne his faculties so meek, hath been
So clear in his great office, that his virtues
Will plead like angels, trumpet-tounged, against
The deep damnation of his taking-off;
And pity, like a naked new-born babe,
Striding the blast, or Heaven's cherubin, horsed
Upon the sightless couriers of the air,
Shall blow the horrid deed in every eye,
That tears shall drown the wind. I have no spur
To prick the sides of my intent, but only
Vaulting ambition, which o'erleaps itself,
And falls on th'other –

Scene 7

A room in **Macbeth's** *castle. A* **Butler** *and several* **Waiters** *cross, carrying dishes of food. Then* **Macbeth** *enters. He is thinking about the proposed murder of* **King Duncan**.

Macbeth If we could get away with the deed after it's done, then the quicker it were done, the better. If the murder had no consequences, and his death ensured success...If, when I strike the blow, that would be the end of it – here, right here, on this side of eternity – we'd willingly chance the life to come. But usually, we get what's coming to us here on earth. We teach the art of bloodshed, then become the victims of our own lessons. This evenhanded justice makes us swallow our own poison. [*Pause*] Duncan is here on double trust: first, because I'm his kinsman and his subject (both good arguments against the deed); then, because I'm his host, who should protect him from his murderer–not bear the knife. Besides, this Duncan has used his power so gently, he's been so incorruptible his great office, that his virtues will plead like angels, their tongues trumpeting the damnable horror of his murder. And pity, like a naked newborn babe or Heaven's avenging angels riding the winds, will cry the deed to everyone so that tears will blind the eye. I've nothing to spur me on but high-leaping ambition, which can often bring about one's downfall.

Shakespeare is Made Easy for these titles:

As You Like It (978-0-7641-4272-7) $6.99, *Can$8.50*
Hamlet (978-0-8120-3638-1) $6.95, *NCR*
Henry IV, Part One (978-0-8120-3585-8) $7.99, *NCR*
Julius Caesar (978-0-8120-3573-5) $6.99, *NCR*
King Lear (978-0-8120-3637-4) $6.99, *NCR*
Macbeth (978-0-8120-3571-1) $6.99, *NCR*
The Merchant of Venice (978-0-8120-3570-4) $6.99, *NCR*
A Midsummer Night's Dream (978-0-8120-3584-1) $6.99, *NCR*
Much Ado About Nothing (978-0-7641-4178-2) $6.99, *Can$8.50*
Othello (978-0-7641-2058-9) $6.95, *Can$8.50*
Romeo & Juliet (978-0-8120-3572-8) $6.99, *NCR*
The Taming of the Shrew (978-0-7641-4190-4) $6.99, *Can$8.50*
The Tempest (978-0-8120-3603-9) $6.95, *NCR*
Twelfth Night (978-0-8120-3604-6) $6.99, *NCR*

To order visit
www.barronseduc.com
or your local book store

A simplified modern translation appears side-by-side with the original Elizabethan text...plus there's helpful background material, study questions, and other aids to better grades.

Yes, up-to-date language now makes it easier to score well on tests *and* enjoy the ageless beauty of the master's works.

Barron's Educational Series, Inc.
250 Wireless Blvd.
Hauppauge, N.Y. 11788
Order toll-free: 1-800-645-3476

Prices subject to change without notice.

In Canada:
Georgetown Book Warehouse
34 Armstrong Ave.
Georgetown, Ontario L7G 4R9
Canadian orders: 1-800-247-7160

Each book: paperback
NCR = No Canadian Rights

(#16) R 5/10

". . . as close, as word for word, as any translation of *The Canterbury Tales*."

—*The New Yorker* magazine

Chaucer's Canterbury Tales (Selected)

An Interlinear Translation, 3rd Edition

Geoffrey Chaucer,
Translated by Vincent F. Hopper,
Edited by Andrew Galloway

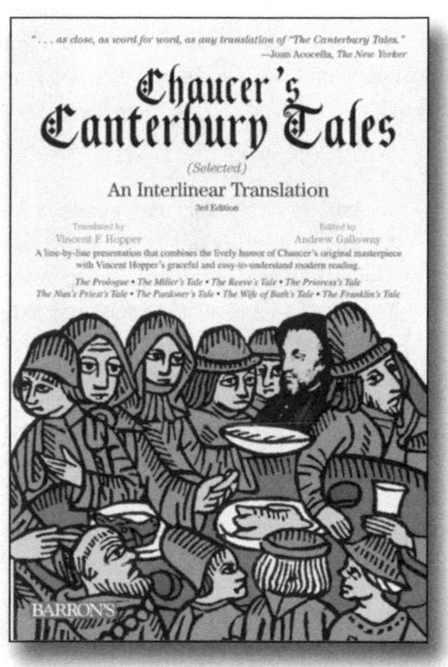

Meet poet Geoffrey Chaucer's immortal storytellers—the comically bawdy Miller . . . the genial and lusty Wife of Bath . . . and many others. A little more than 600 years ago, when Chaucer wrote his masterpiece, he used the English language dialect that was standard in his day. Though a rich, vital language, it's very different from the English we speak today. Vincent Hopper's critically praised translation of *The Canterbury Tales* is presented here with an enlightening introduction by pre-Renaissance literary scholar Andrew Galloway. This fine edition offers readers—

- The vigor, liveliness, and humor of Chaucer's original Middle English poetry, interspersed line-by-line with a modern, easy-to-understand translation.
- An ideal classroom text for students of English literature.

Here is an attractive and approachable version of a richly entertaining literary classic, suitable for both students and the general reader.

Paperback, ISBN 978-1-4380-0013-8
$14.99, ***Canada $16.99***

Prices subject to change without notice.

———To order———
Available at your local book store
or visit **www.barronseduc.com**

Barron's Educational Series, Inc.
250 Wireless Blvd.
Hauppauge, N.Y. 11788
Order toll-free: 1-800-645-3476
Order by fax: 1-631-434-3217

In Canada:
Georgetown Book Warehouse
34 Armstrong Ave.
Georgetown, Ontario L7G 4R9
Canadian orders: 1-800-247-7160
Order by fax: 1-800-887-1594

(#229) R10/11